Intermediate
Language Skills
READING

Frank Heyworth

HODDER AND STOUGHTON

LONDON SYDNEY AUCKLAND TORONTO

ISBN 0 340 25609 5

First published 1982
Second impression 1984

Photo Typeset by Macmillan India Ltd, Bangalore.

Printed in Hong Kong for Hodder and Stoughton
Educational, a division of Hodder and Stoughton Ltd,
Mill Road, Dunton Green, Sevenoaks, Kent, by
Colorcraft Ltd.

Intermediate
Language Skills
READING

Contents

Acknowledgements

The publisher would like to thank the following for permission to reproduce or adapt copyright material:

The Illustrated Weekly of India
The Observer Foreign News Service
Her Majesty's Stationery Office
Heinemann Educational Books
Methuen & Co Ltd
Mr Gary Yerkey
Mr Gene Zelazny
Ms Marion Kaplan
Penguin Books Ltd
Christian Aid
Zomo Publicity
The Unesco Courier
New Scientist
Spare Rib
Jonathan Cape Ltd

In the case of *How long does it take to earn a kilogramme of rice?*, it has not proved possible to trace the copyright owners, but full acknowledgement will be made in later printings if the publishers are notified as to whom they should contact.

Foreword

Intermediate Language Skills: Reading is the fif-
teenth book for language learners and teachers
produced by teachers and materials writers from the
Foundation for European Language and Educational
Centres. Some have been designed for teachers' use,
others for direct classroom use by students, but all
have attempted innovatory approaches. This reading
skills book is no exception, and is directed to the new
generation of language learners who want to go
beyond acquisition of a system of structures to the
development of strategies for processing and using
language communicatively. It is innovative in the
way it puts reading activity firmly in a communicative context and in the encouragement it gives to
students to use their intelligence and creativity in the
reading process. It was developed in Iran for use with
students in urgent need of study skills, but we think its
approach is one that can provide more general
relevance and even serve as a model for intelligent
and lively learning of language skills.

E. J. C. Waespi
Director, Eurocentres

Notes for the teacher

What this book sets out to do

To develop students' skills as readers. This means developing their ability to *understand, interpret, process, and use* what is contained in reading matter and in the diagrams and illustrations that accompany it.

The book does *not* use reading texts as a way of teaching grammar and structures or as a pretext for drills or exercises on general grammar and lexis.

In order to read effectively it is necessary:

- to be aware of the nature of what you are reading, i.e. to distinguish between different types of text.
- to be aware of the purpose you have in reading – to pass the time in a train, to study for an exam, to find out at what time your train is leaving, to support your point of view in an argument, to pick out information for a particular purpose, to satisfy curiosity, to assess a proposal . . .
- to decide on a reading approach or strategy suitable for your purpose.
- to be able to use different reading strategies – close reading, skimming, scanning, memorising . . .
- to be able to understand the different ways used to link the different parts of a text to each other to give cohesion and coherence to the text.
- to be able to select and process the information so that it is in a form usable for your purposes – notes, a diagram, sketches, or some other form of speech and writing.

The activities proposed in *Intermediate Language Skills: Reading* are designed to lead students to an awareness of these skills and some part of the way to being able to use them well.

Each unit except units 9 and 14, which are applications of earlier work, consists of *seven parts* which are intended to let the student go systematically through the basic activities involved in reading.

Section One: Situation

Here the reading situation is described – who the reader is, the context and setting in which he is reading, his attitudes and intentions at the moment of reading; outside the classroom it is very seldom that anyone reads without a precise reason or at least setting. In order to reproduce this situation in the lesson the student is asked to play the role of someone who would need to deal with the reading passage for a real purpose. Section One provides an opportunity for students to discuss the *purpose* of their reading, and to talk about the *strategy* they would use to approach it.

Section Two: Think it over

Again in 'real' reading it is very rare to start reading something without more or less clear ideas about what one expects to find in the passage. Indeed many forms of reading involve a sort of internal dialogue between reader and text, where the reader compares the content of the passage with his own previous knowledge and opinions and decides whether to accept or reject it. One of the skills of rapid reading is the ability to predict what is going to come next, and a source of this is one's predictions about the content. (Another source is of course knowledge of the grammar of written English and its signalling devices.) In Section Two students can talk over in general what they know and think about the subject in question so that they come to it prepared in the way they would be in native language reading and therefore prepared to enter a dialogue with it.

Section Three: Text

Here the text is reproduced – if possible in its original form and presentation. All the texts are authentic with some occasional slight condensation in order to present a coherent piece of language. They have been chosen mainly from newspaper and magazine sources and are concerned with contemporary life and society. No literary texts have been used. An attempt has been used to provide texts from international rather than purely British sources, and there are passages from American, Indian and European books, newspapers and magazines. At the end of each text is a question requiring students to identify the text type – popular or learned, newspaper or book . . .

Section Four: *Language work*

This section is printed opposite the text and contains work on the vocabulary and structures necessary to understand the text. The emphasis is on activities which allow students to develop skills – like how to guess the meaning of an unknown word from its context or form, or the general uses of reference in written English – enabling them to deal with other texts outside the classroom with a greater chance of success. In some units this section contains work on interpreting the writer's attitude towards the subject and some of the ways in which this is signalled to the reader. The exercises aim to help the student to understand the text as he goes along by asking explicitly the kind of questions he will ask himself in out-of-class reading. It tries to establish a *dialogue* between student and text.

Section Five: *Overall understanding*

The activities proposed in Section Five treat the passage as a whole – whereas Section Four is word and sentence based. It refers back to the work of Sections One and Two in which reading purpose and expectations have been discussed and examines how the information in the passage can be processed and transformed to meet the aims we have defined before reading. It relates the action of reading back to reader, setting and purpose.

Section Six: *Using your reading*

This section reinforces the major aim of the book – to deal with reading as a purposeful activity – by relating to a task which requires the *use* of the information acquired during the reading. This can be in the form of a discussion, or talk to be prepared, or a role play to be carried out, or in some units, written work – making lecture notes, producing a sketch or plan of action. The role situation introduced in Section One is the setting for the *communicative task* which is set.

Section Seven: *Summary*

Each unit closes with a summary of the reading skills covered in the preceding work and can serve as a reference point for both teacher and students while working through the book and once the course is complete.

Using the book

It is recommended that you allow three teaching hours for each unit of the book:

Session One for dealing with setting up the situation, talking through it, defining the reading strategy and approach, talking about the type of text and reading through the passage.

Session Two for dealing with the language work and overall understanding.

Session Three for preparing and carrying out the task in Section Six *Using Your Reading*.

Teachers will clearly want to integrate *pair* and *group work* into the reading lesson, and the discussion elements in Session One, the work on overall understanding in Lesson Two and the preparation for the task are well suited to this. If there is a guided or self-study element to the course it should also be possible for students to attempt the second session independently.

Other teaching methods which have been found to work when the material was being tested are:

Setting time limits for skimming and scanning exercises.

Putting *skeleton outlines* of the text on an overhead projector transparency and giving students a time limit for filling in the details in note form.

Dividing the class into two groups one of which reads the passage while the other, without looking at the passage, prepares questions to elicit the content. The two halves of the class can then be mixed up to give the questions and answers – this to be followed by close reading to see whether the *information gap* has been successfully filled. It is probably best if both sides are given a role identity in this activity in order to maintain the idea of purposeful reading.

Throughout the book, reading is treated as an intelligent activity and teachers are advised to spend time discussing the *why*s and *how*s of reading with their students. The students' notes on page x immediately before the first reading passage are intended as an introduction to get students thinking about what they are learning.

To the student

The reading activities in this book are designed to help you improve your reading in English. Reading used to be considered the passive part of learning a language, but in this book we try to involve you actively in the process.

To read well you need first to decide on your reading purpose – *why* you are reading a particular passage – for information, enjoyment, making plans, confirming your opinions . . .

Next you must decide on *how* you are going to read it – your reading *approach* or *strategy* – quickly, carefully, to remember all the information or to select just the small part you want . . .

Reading is a kind of dialogue between the reader and the writer – he adds to what you already know or changes your opinion or knowledge about a question. Therefore it's useful to discuss what you know already.

During your reading you need to develop some *skills* – how to guess the meanings of words from their context; how to recognise the links between the different parts of the passage; how to separate the facts from the opinions . . .

The exercises in the book try to give you practice in doing the things you need to do to be a good reader. Of course, in reality, *you* decide *what* you are going to read and *why* you are going to read it, but this cannot be included in the book. So each unit of the book has a first section called situation in which you are asked to imagine you are a particular person and to decide *why* and *how* he or she would read the passage. This is to provide a context like the one you will do your own reading in. The situation is repeated in the last section of each unit where you are asked to perform a task in which you use and apply what you have read.

Frank Heyworth
September 1981

1 Interpol

Situation

You have a job as a programme researcher in the drama and series department of OTV, a commercial television company. Your boss, the producer Harry Gregg, wants to get away from the usual series of detective stories or films about police or gangsters in London or New York:

> 'What I want is a story about *real* people with a *real* background: you know, based on things that really happen. And I'd like to get a new setting, like Africa or India, instead of staying in Britain or the States. Now you go and find me something about the problems of crime in Lagos or Delhi or Singapore. I'd like you to come back with ideas for a series of documentary adventures – with human interest, not sensational violence.'

During your researches you found this article in the *Illustrated Weekly of India* . . .

Think it over

You made notes on your talk with Harry Gregg:

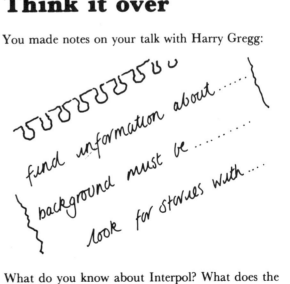

find information about......
background must be.........
look for stories with....

What do you know about Interpol? What does the name suggest about its activities? What kind of crimes would you expect an international police force to deal with?

WHAT DO YOU KNOW ALREADY?

WHAT IS YOUR READING PURPOSE?

In all of these units you are going to work on reading with a purpose. The description of the situation will allow you to decide on your approach to the reading passage. In this unit you are a programme researcher and you see the title *What is International Crime?*

HOW ARE YOU GOING TO READ?

– read the article quickly noting every fact
– 'skim' – read quickly to get the main points
– 'scan' – glance at quickly looking for specific information
– read in a relaxed way to pass the time.

Use the reading approach you have decided on to read the article. If you decide to scan or skim, read the advice on this on page 5.

Text

What is international crime?

1973 was the year of Interpol's fiftieth anniversary, and today it continues to develop and expand, currently with a hundred and twenty-four member countries, including India.

A policeman's first reaction when he hears something described as a crime is to find out whether the law has been broken. Where there is no law, there can be no crimes – only anti-social behaviour or offences against moral and religious standards. The first question, therefore, is: Are there any international crimes, legally speaking? And the answer is No – for several reasons.

In the first place there is no international penal code or body of international law defining international crimes or offences. Secondly, national penal codes are only valid within a particular country. Efforts have been made to have certain activities universally recognised as criminal. The fact remains that there are no international laws listing or defining international crime. How then, you may ask, is it possible to have an international police force? It has been accepted by the countries affiliated to Interpol that any criminal activity which has an international bearing, either in itself or because of the character of the offender, should be considered an international crime.

This can be illustrated by a recent case in India. A British national, posing as a correspondent of a leading British daily, came to India. He evinced considerable interest in the jewellery markets of Delhi and seemed intent on buying large quantities of expensive jewellery.

One shopkeeper, keen to sell his wares, obligingly made a deal with him for 22,000 rupees; the only difficulty was the mode of payment. The foreigner issued two cheques drawn on the Bangkok branch of the Bank of America, which the shopkeeper accepted, impressed by the customer's prosperous ways. The foreigner had, however, issued fake cheques and he lost no time in leaving the country with his precious possession.

The cheques bounced. The shopkeeper went to the local police. Interpol, Delhi, on request from the local police, promptly got in touch with Interpol, London, and learnt that the international swindler had been arrested there, convicted and sentenced to two years' imprisonment for theft as well as for issuing worthless cheques.

It came to light that he had twenty-seven convictions for similar offences. Interpol asked Britain to extradite him and he was brought to Delhi and sentenced to one year's rigorous imprisonment and fined 2000 rupees.

Abridged and adapted from an article in the *Illustrated Weekly of India*, 26.11.78.

Language work

A Vocabulary in context

How can we find out the meanings of words we don't know without having to look at a dictionary each time? One way is through looking at the context of the word, assessing all the information you know from the words you do understand. For example, you may not know the meaning of the word 'swindler' in line 67; but you do know that it is used to describe the man in the story who is a criminal – so you can guess that it is probably another word for a kind of criminal. You can even be more specific: what kind of criminal is he? Not a murderer or a train robber, but someone who cheats or tricks people. And this is what a swindler is – a kind of criminal who cheats people.

Try to guess the meanings of the following words using the context to help you:

1   *valid* (line 24) – think of the meaning of the whole sentence – *valid* can be guessed from this.
2   *affiliated* (line 34) – think of '124 member countries'. If you're affiliated to an organisation you're a . . . of it.
3   *posing* (line 42) – is the man really a journalist? No, he is . . . to be one.
4   *evinced* (line 44) – what other word could fit into 'he . . . interest'?
5   *wares* (line 50) – what do shopkeepers do? They sell . . .
6   *fake* (line 59) – do you think the cheques were genuine, real ones?
7   *bounced* (line 62) – did the shopkeeper receive payment on the cheques? No, they . . .
8   *extradite* (line 75) – the British authorities sent him out of the country to India, so . . .
9   *rigorous* (line 77) – will prison be a pleasant experience?

B Vocabulary building

A second way of working out what words probably mean is to think of the form of the word to see if it reminds you of other words you know. *Penal* in line 20 is probably new to you but you will probably be able to connect it with *penalty* and guess that *penal code* is a system which sets out which activities are against the law and will be punished.

Even if you didn't know the word *anti-social*, you will be able to work out the meaning from the prefix *anti-*, meaning *against*, and *social* you will link with *society* to get the sense of 'anti-social' as an adjective describing actions against society.

Try the same technique on the following words (if you don't already know them):

1   *universally* (line 26) means . . . linked to . . .
2   *intent* (line 46) means . . . linked to . . .
3   *imprisonment* (lines 69–70) means . . . linked to . . .
4   *worthless* (line 71) means . . . links . . . and . . .

C Comprehension

1   What do you expect to learn from the article after you have read the title?
2   The text gives two definitions of crime – one for ordinary people, and one for policemen:
    Ordinary people consider a crime is . . . while for policemen the definition of a crime is . . . Why is the policeman's meaning different?
3   What difficulty for the activities of an international police force is raised in lines 19–30?
4   What are the reasons for this difficulty?
5   How is this difficulty overcome by Interpol? Member countries have agreed that . . .
6   This can be illustrated by a recent case in India – what does this mean? (lines 40–1)
7   This is the story of a crime:
    a)   Who was the criminal?
    b)   What did he do?
    c)   Who did he pretend to be?
    d)   Why did the shopkeeper accept the cheques?
    e)   How did Interpol help?
    f)   What punishment did the criminal receive?

General question

How does the story help the reader to understand the question asked in the title of the text? It is an example of how . . .

Overall understanding

1   Do you think the author of the text is: (a) a journalist? (b) a lawyer? (c) a policeman? (d) a criminal? Explain your choice.

2 Is the text meant for the general public or for specialists?

3 As a programme researcher, which parts of the text would you find most interesting – the details about the way Interpol works, or the story about the criminal? Or both? Or neither?

4 As a programme researcher you would obviously want to take some notes on the passage – but only of the things you feel would be of use to you for the job you have been given. These would probably be of two kinds: (a) background information about Interpol and how it works (b) ideas for the story.

Remember that in note form you do not need to put in the articles or the full forms of verbs. Instead of *A confidence trickster was caught with the help of Interpol information about his previous crime* you can put *trickster caught by Interpol info on former crimes.*

Choose what you would note down from the article and write it in note form.

5 Somebody sees you reading the article and says, *What's that you're reading?* Give a brief answer – *Oh, it's about how . . . This is illustrated by a story about . . .*

> NOTES ON INTERPOL ARTICLE
>
> Background Information:
>
> 1 . . . .
> 2 . . . .
> 3 . . . .
> 4 . . . .
>
> Story details:
>
> 1 . . . .
> 2 . . . .
> 3 . . . .
> 4 . . . .

Using your reading

The article gave you an idea for a TV series. Write a note to your boss explaining it. One possibility – a series using the background of Interpol in India – say why it would be interesting, who the main characters in the story could be, where the story would take place; give some ideas for further adventures. Another possibility – a series about international criminals and swindlers, what they do, how they work, the harmful effects of their crimes; give ideas for other stories.

You could begin: *I think we could do a story about Interpol in India.* (Why? Background . . . Characters . . . Setting . . .)

How to scan

Scanning is a reading skill you use when you want to check quickly whether a text you are reading contains information you need. Here are some tips on how to do it:

1   Think of some key words connected with the information you need – look quickly down the page to see if you can spot any of them. If you do, read the sentences around them to check if it's what you need.
2   Look for chapter headings/paragraph headings – words in bold type/words underlined. They give you a lot of quick information about the contents of reading matter.
3   If it's in a book, look at the list of contents and the indexes.

You can use the same techniques to *skim*, that is, to read something quickly to get the main points.

To practise these skills try giving yourself a very short time (say 30 seconds) to look at a page and see how much of the most important meaning you can get.

Summary

In this unit you have worked on selecting relevant details from an article; on how to guess the probable meanings of words from their context or from their form. You have seen how examples can be used to illustrate a general point.

2 About Chinese

Situation

Stieg, Maria and Chantal are all studying English in Britain. One day in the coffee-break they had a discussion about learning languages and about which languages were the most difficult to learn:

STIEG: I think French is the hardest language I know – all the rules about agreements of adjectives and participles.

CHANTAL: It's not nearly as difficult as German. Have you ever looked at a German grammar? It's frightening.

MARIA: Anyway, all European languages must be easy compared to Chinese. Think of learning thousands of different characters all written the wrong way round. It would take years even to begin to read properly.

STIEG: I'm not sure, you know. They say Chinese grammar is very simple, and the writing's a system of pictures. Once you know how the system works it would be easy.

CHANTAL: I don't think you're right about the writing. It used to be pictures but now it's much more complicated, and the writing goes from top to bottom . . .

In fact none of them really knew much about Chinese; as they were near the school library they went in and found a book called *About Chinese* . . .

今晚係唐餐定係

張 張 屋 我 要 條 餐
先 太 有 怕 熨 褲 定
生 太 冷 我 吓 唔 係

WHAT IS YOUR READING PURPOSE?

Note any questions you would like to get answers to by reading the passage. Do you want to know *everything* about Chinese? Do you need to memorise what you learn? How will you approach your reading task?

– close reading to understand all the details?
– skimming to get the general meaning of the passage?
– scanning to pick out particular points?

Think it over

What do you think about the students' discussion? Who do you think was right about Chinese writing? How much do you *know* about Chinese? What would you expect to be the difficulties involved in learning it?

What exactly is the information the three students want to find out from the book about Chinese?

WHAT DO YOU KNOW ALREADY?

Text

In your first reading of this passage try to scan to see if it contains some of the information you are looking for. In one minute look through quickly to see if any key words appear about the way in which Chinese people write – these words could include *direction, left to right, backwards* . . . note in which paragraphs you find them.

Chinese Script

A common belief about Chinese characters is that they are pictures written down back to front. This is quite wrong. But it may be useful to examine the separate parts of this belief in order to clarify what Chinese script really is, and to show that, although Chinese writing is difficult, there are certain lines of approach open to us.

In the first place, the system of Chinese writing has at least five separate elements. Picture writing may be involved in all of these, just as *sound-painting* is involved in some words in most European languages. But to say that Chinese characters are all drawings of things is like saying that all English words are like *cuckoo* or *splash*. Very few characters today can still be seen as pictures.

Secondly, taking *written down back to front* to refer to the direction followed when writing a Chinese sentence, there is no absolute rule on this point. For the last decade, Peking has wisely imposed *left to right* as the form for both handwriting and printing. Elsewhere, and even in China among older people, the most usual handwriting direction is in downward columns, starting from the right margin.

Thirdly, it is incorrect to say that the individual character is written backwards, that is, right to left in order of making the pen strokes. Left to right is the rule for most letters.

The notion of characters as pictures does, however, give an historical starting point from which to approach the five different types of Chinese characters. Certainly the earliest characters were pictures. Their first appearance in about 1400 B. C. shows a high proportion of recognisable drawings: ⊙ for sun (now 日), 𝄞 for moon (now 月). But even at this early date it was impossible to express everything by pictures and to represent ideas and concepts symbolism began to be used.

From pp. 34–5, *About Chinese*, by Robert Newnham, published by Penguin Books Ltd.

Language work

A Comprehension

1 A *common belief* = a lot of people think. What is the *common belief* here?

2 Is this belief (a) correct? (b) mistaken?

3 Why does the writer think it is useful to examine this idea people have about Chinese writing?
   (a) because it makes Chinese less difficult?
   (b) because it contains some elements of truth?
   (c) because looking at the belief helps to explain what Chinese writing really is?

4 According to the writer, Chinese characters are . . . pictures:

(a) always (b) sometimes (c) very rarely (d) never

In Chinese, picture characters *show* the meaning of the word. In English, words like 'cuckoo' and 'splash' give the *sound* of the word. Can you think of similar words in English and your own language?

5 What are the different directions in which Chinese is written?

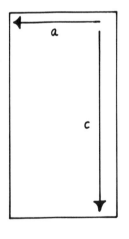 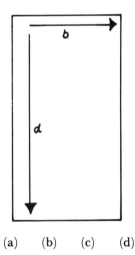

(a)   (b)   (c)   (d)

In Communist China?
Outside China?
By old Chinese people?

6 In 1400 BC
   a) All Chinese writing was made up of pictures.
   b) Pictures were used in writing to represent objects.
   c) Chinese writing had already abandoned the picture system.

B Linking paragraphs

To read effectively you must of course understand the meaning of the sentences and paragraphs you read. You must also understand how the sentences and paragraphs are linked so that the passage has unity and is not simply a list of separate sentences. In this passage there are two kinds of link signalled by the writer:

1) Listing – the writer gives a list of common beliefs about Chinese and uses expressions like *in the first place*, *secondly*, etc. He could also have used words like *then* and *next* to show he is moving from one point to the next.

2) Indicating a contrast – words and expressions like *however, on the other hand, but* are used to show that what comes next is *not* a continuation of a list, but a *change* in the writer's direction of thought – he is telling the reader that there are points which may contrast with or contradict what he has just said.

In this text the writer announces in his first paragraph that he is going to examine people's common beliefs about Chinese writing.

1 How many points does he make about this belief? 1, 2, 3, 4?

2 What words does he use to indicate that he is ending one point and beginning the next one?
   1 In the first place.
   2 . . .
   3 . . .
   4 The notion of characters as pictures does, *however*, give . . .

3 Why does the writer indicate the change from one point to the next by the use of *however* rather than *next* or *fourthly*?

Peace

The English word consists of separate shapes we call letters which represent the sounds we make when we say the word. The Chinese word consists of two small drawings. One is the drawing of a roof (which is the Chinese word roof) and one is a drawing of a woman (which is the Chinese word for woman). Put a woman under a roof and you have a home and so the idea of Peace.

Originally all Chinese words were tiny drawings — some simple, some complex.

Here are some of them.

Here are two words:
the Chinese word for peace
and the English word.

Child

Man

Protect

Can you see that the man with his arm over the child comes to form the idea of protection?

What happens in this one?

Hand

Eye

?

Originally then, a Chinese word was a picture or an image of what it represented.

Our written language is totally different. A word like peace is a sound, not two drawings of real things like a woman and a roof. But we can bring pictures into the mind of the reader through images. We can say that Peace is a very old woman resting by the fire or that Peace is a white dove or that Peace is the lamb and fox sleeping together.

In each of these examples I am giving you a picture, or an image — of Peace.

From *English Broadsheets* published by Heinemann Educational Books Ltd.

Overall understanding

1 Here are some of the statements Stieg, Maria and Chantal made about Chinese writing. Use the table to indicate whether the statements are true, partly true, mistaken, or not mentioned in the text.

1 Chinese writing is a system of pictures.
2 The writing goes from right to left.
3 You draw the characters starting from the left.
4 The writing goes from top to bottom.
5 There are thousands of different characters
6 Chinese writing used to be a system of pictures but this is no longer true
7 Chinese grammar is easy

true	partly true	mistaken	not mentioned

2 Imagine you have overheard the conversation between the three students; use the information in the text to correct their mistaken impressions – *No, you're all wrong. In fact, Chinese writing is . . .*

3 Do you think the text is taken from a book for the general public, or a book for specialists?

Using your reading

Use the information in the text and in the illustrations of how Chinese can express ideas in pictures to prepare a short talk to the class with the title:

The use of pictures in Chinese writing

Don't forget to indicate that not all Chinese writing is made of pictures and that there are other elements involved.

Summary

In this unit you have worked on scanning to find particular pieces of information from a text and on understanding the ways in which ideas are linked from one paragraph to another.

3 How long does it take to earn a kilogramme of rice?

Situation

– I can't understand how anyone can live in Switzerland. The cost of living is at least twice as high as in Britain.

– You don't understand. It all depends on how much you're paid. If you have a Swiss salary the cost of living in Geneva is just the same as in London; in fact it's probably lower because there isn't as much inflation.

– But that's ridiculous. A cup of coffee costs almost five times as much. The only places in Europe where it's cheaper than Britain are Portugal and Turkey.

– What do you mean, cheaper? It's a matter of the exchange rate. If you try to live on a Portuguese salary you'll find everything's very expensive. The inflation there last year was enormous.

How *can* you measure the cost of living? What do you mean when you say one country has a higher standard of living than another?

North-South Gap Widens

By our Political Correspondent

A report published today by the Government's economic "think-tank" shows that the difference in living standards between the developed and the developing countries is growing. The survey is based on the cost of several basic foodstuffs and the rate of inflation and over forty countries were investigated.

While the West has been badly hit by oil-based inflation over the last three years the effects on the poorer nations have been devastating.

WHAT IS YOUR READING PURPOSE?

Here is a passage about costs of living in different countries. How would you read it if: (a) You had just had the conversation above? (b) If you had been offered a job which involved spending six months in India? (c) If you were a student of economics doing a project on living conditions in developing countries?

1 Scanning to see if there is any information relevant to your needs?
2 Reading through rapidly for general interest?
3 Reading carefully to understand and evaluate?

Think it over

What do you know about the cost of living in your country? Has it been stable recently, or has there been a lot of inflation? How does it compare with other countries you know? Which countries do you consider as being 'cheap' and which 'expensive'? What are the difficulties involved in making comparisons of this kind? What criteria could you use to measure whether one country has a higher cost of living or a better standard of living than another?

WHAT DO YOU KNOW ALREADY?

Text

Read the passage twice:
1 Rapidly for general interest – in five minutes. After this reading, discuss in class (a) the general theme of the passage (b) as many details as you remember from the first reading.
2 Read carefully to answer the questions in sections 4 and 5.

How long does it take to earn a kilogramme of rice?

An Indian driver or carpenter has to work about two hours to buy a kilogramme of rice while his counterpart in Austria, the Netherlands and Switzerland need work only fifteen minutes for it.

In Botswana, Greece and Romania, forty minutes of driving earns a kilogramme of rice. This is part of the data collected by the International Labour Office on hourly rates in forty-one occupations and consumer prices for a sample of household items in about 100 countries.

It is realised that international comparisons are difficult because of the different criteria used by different countries to gather statistics. Some items may be in great demand by workers in one country and not so much in another. But generally the data gives an idea of the value of the basic pay received for an hour's work in various parts of the world in terms of food purchasing power. Take a baker in Syria or Botswana. He has to work almost two hours at the oven to earn one kilogramme of bread, but a Canadian or Belgian baker could earn the same loaf by working just ten minutes.

Sugar is considered a luxury in Burma, where the majority of workers have to put in at least thirteen hours' work before they can earn one kilogramme of it. But the same stuff could be had for ninety minutes' work in Benin and Nigeria, thirty minutes labour in Guadeloupe, and for a mere ten minutes stint in Mexico.

Most of the wage earners in the market-economy countries, the study shows, can buy one kilogramme of sugar with less than twenty minutes' wages. And for Austrian, Bermudan and Canadian bakers and carpenters an hour's wage could fetch ten kilogrammes of sugar.

In fact there is an enormous range in the working time necessary to earn various commodities. Butter can 'cost' up to three hours' work, but only requires twenty minutes in Australia and New Zealand. A carpenter in the USA earns enough to pay fourteen dozen eggs in the time it would take his counterpart in Portugal or Fiji to earn a dozen, and if a British carpenter feels like a litre of beer it will take him forty-five minutes to earn it – three times as long as a worker in the Netherlands.

WHAT KIND OF TEXT?

Do you think that this passage comes from (a) a book? (b) a newspaper? (c) a report for the United Nations? Is it for the general public or specialists?

Language work

A Comprehension

1   What is being compared in the first paragraph? The difference between . . .

2   In what country does rice cost most in terms of working time?

3   In what countries does it cost least? ·

4   Complete: In India it takes . . . times as long to earn . . . as in Botswana.

5   What is the source of the information contained in the text?

6   What information has been collected:
    (a)   concerning wages? – the basic pay for . . .
    (b)   in how many countries?
    (c)   for which professions?
    (d)   concerning prices? for what kinds of goods?

7   The text *qualifies* the information—it tells the reader, that not everything in the data can be considered as giving a full picture of the cost of living in different countries.

    What are the reasons for the qualifications? Why is it difficult to compare some of the information provided?

    Because different countries (a) . . . (b) . . .

    In spite of the qualifications the writer thinks the study is a useful one because it gives an idea of . . .

8   Line 30–1 – Does this mean that the price of sugar is the same in Syria as in Botswana? . . .

9   Fill in the chart below to give information about the relative prices of sugar in different countries.

10   Which countries are referred to as 'market-economy countries'?

B Comparison

The text contains a large number of comparisons between countries. Notice the different ways in which the comparisons are indicated:

Lines 1–4. An Indian driver or carpenter has to work . . . *while* his counterpart in Austria . . .

Lines 21–4. Some items may be in great demand by workers in one country and *not so much* in another.

Lines 30–5. The baker in Syria or Botswana has to work almost two hours to earn a kilogram of bread, *but* a Canadian or Belgian baker could earn *the same loaf* in . . .

Lines 68–72. It will take a British worker *three times as long* to earn enough to buy a litre of beer *as* a worker in the Netherlands. Remember: the same *as;* twice *as long as; much more* expensive *than.*

How long does it take to earn:
1 dozen eggs in the USA?
1 litre of beer in Amsterdam?
6 eggs in Fiji?
3 kgs of butter in Australia?

    If you have sufficient information, put the exact time needed. If not, express in terms of comparisons, using expressions like 'as long as', 'twice/three times as long as'.

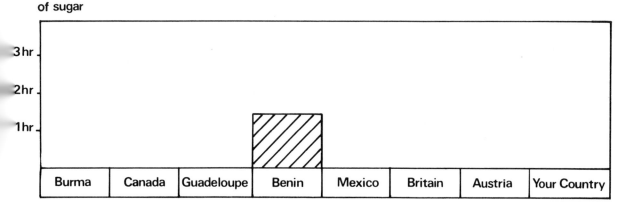

Time taken to earn 1kg of sugar

	Burma	Canada	Guadeloupe	Benin	Mexico	Britain	Austria	Your Country

3 hr
2 hr
1 hr

C Words and context

1 Try to work out from the context what the word *counterpart* means . . .
2 *Data* is another word for . . .
3 If you choose a 'sample' of something, you choose (a) as many as possible (b) a small number (c) a typical selection (d) a wide variety.
4 A *criterion* (pl. *criteria*) is a . . . on which you can base a judgment. *food purchasing power* is the . . . with a given amount of money.
Data, criteria, sample, purchasing power, item, statistics are words likely to be found when you are reading about subjects liie . . .

Overall understanding

1 Does the text answer the question *how can you compare the cost of living and standards of living in different countries*?
It claims that one valid criterion is . . . because this . . .

Do you agree that this is a valid way of judging differences? Could you make any suggestions for improving the comparison? . . .

2 Here are some generalisations. Which of them can be supported by the information provided in the text?

(a) Food is cheaper in European countries than in the rest of the world.
(b) People in developing countries have to work longer to earn the basic necessities of living.
(c) The cost of living in Mexico is very low.
(d) The Burmese economy is probably in a difficult situation.
(e) Dutchmen drink more than the English do.
(f) The study contains a full account of differences in the cost of living in 100 countries.
(g) Carpenters in the USA are very well paid.
(h) Africans mentioned in the study earn more food purchasing power in an hour than the Asians.

3 What general conclusion about the range and distribution of wealth in the world could be drawn from the text?

Using your reading

Try to collect data of the same kind as is contained in the text about the country you live in or another country you know well.

– What is the basic hourly wage for workers of different categories?
– What basic commodities can be bought in return for the hourly wage?
– How long does it take to earn a kg of butter?
– A loaf of bread?
– A small car?
– To pay the rent for a three-room flat?

Use the information to compare costs and standards of living with the results found by other students. Find the information you need to complete the chart on the following page.

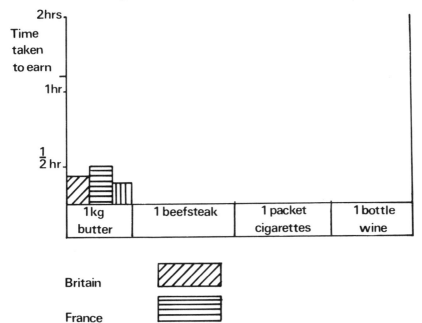

Britain

France

Germany

Summary

In this unit you have seen expressions of comparison,
sorted out detailed information; organised some of it
into a chart, and you have made generalisations from
the facts given in the text.

4 Accidents

Situation You work in an industrial company in which people work with high speed machines. Although company regulations about safe working are very strict there are still a number of accidents on the machines every year. Your boss has told you to investigate the situation, and to write a report on the causes of accidents and on what can be done to prevent them. The first thing you do is to go and observe the work and the machines, but you also decide to read some articles about the causes of accidents in general and find this article in a women's magazine.

BUILDING WITHOUT ACCIDENTS

Over 40,000 accidents occur in building and construction work each year — nearly 250 men are killed outright or die from their injuries. At this rate, every man in the construction industry can expect to be injured twice during his working life and one in every hundred will die in a building accident. The risk of a fatal accident is about three times more in building than in the manufacturing industries.
In addition to the distress caused to men and their families, accidents in building cost the country at least £30 million each year — we cannot afford this or the loss of valuable manpower. This leaflet, prepared in conjunction with the Ministry of Labour, tells you how to reduce the number of accidents on your site.

WHAT IS YOUR READING PURPOSE?

How are you going to approach your reading?
- reading very carefully, noting all the details?
- reading carefully to get the most important general points?
- both of these?
- reading quickly to see if there is anything of interest?

Think it over

Before reading the article, what do you already know about the causes of accidents? Are some people more liable to have accidents than others? Are there times when people are more likely to have an accident than others? Do accidents happen purely by chance?

WHAT DO YOU KNOW ALREADY?

Text

Dr Evelyn Weston looks beyond the accident figures and outlines the conditions that pre-dispose us to injuries and casualties of one kind or another.

Accidents are caused, they don't just happen. The reason may be easy to see: an overloaded tray, a shelf out of reach, a patch of ice on the road. But more often than not there is a chain of events leading up to the calamity – frustration, tiredness or just bad temper – that show what the accident really is, a sort of attack on oneself.

Road accidents, for example, happen frequently after a family row, and we all know people who are accident-prone, so often at odds with themselves and the world that they seem to cause accidents for themselves and others.

Yet this should not make us think that accidents happen to other people. By definition, an accident is something you cannot predict or avoid, and the idea which used to be current, that the majority of road accidents are caused by a minority of criminally careless drivers, is not supported by insur-

ance statistics. These show that most accidents involve ordinary motorists in a moment of carelessness or thoughtlessness.

It is not always clear, either, what sort of conditions make people more likely to have an accident. For instance, the law requires all factories to take safety precautions and most companies have safety committees to make sure the regulations are observed, but still, every day in Britain, some fifty thousand men and women are absent from work due to an accident. These accidents are largely the result of human error or misjudgement – noise and fatigue, boredom or worry are possible factors which contribute to this. Doctors who work in factories have found that those who drink too much, usually people who have a high anxiety level, run three times the normal risk of accidents at work.

WHAT KIND OF TEXT?

Do you think this is a passage (a) from a book (b) from a magazine? Is it for specialists or the general public?

Language work

A Vocabulary

1 Here are some difficult words from the text. Join each one to the right definition:

a accident-prone   argument
b row   disaster
c calamity   steps taken to avoid
d precautions   accidents error
e misjudgement   liable to have accidents

Use the context to help you decide.

2 Adding:

-*ful* is a way of changing a noun into an adjective:
   help----helpful

-*ness* is a way of changing an adjective into a noun:
   helpful----helpfulness

Complete the table

NOUN	ADJECTIVE	NOUN
help	helpful	helpfulness
thought		
care		
—	tired	
		hopefulness

3 After reading the introduction to the passage what do you expect?
(a) An explanation of the immediate causes of accidents?
   or
(b) An account of what makes people liable to have accidents?
The expression *looks beyond* . . . will help you to decide.

B Comprehension

Paragraph 1
Which general statement sums up the paragraph best?
1 Accidents are usually caused by physical factors – like a patch of ice.
2 Accidents are usually caused by psychological factors.

Paragraph 2
This gives two examples of the statement *Accidents are caused by* . . . Summarise the examples –
1 Road accidents are often caused . . .
2 Some people have frequent accidents because . . .

Paragraph 3
The word *yet* at the beginning of a paragraph often gives a warning to the reader: *Because of what I've just written, don't think that* . . .
Some people think that most accidents are caused by a few careless drivers. Is this true? What evidence do we have?

Paragraph 4
Here is a general scheme of what the paragraph says. Rewrite the paragraph in your own words using these headings
General statement: *We do not know exactly* . . .
1 Explanation of general statement
2 Even though there are laws to protect . . .
3 Safety committees are meant to . . .
4 Possible answers to the question implied by 'it is not always clear . . .'
5 Factors which may cause accidents at work are . . .

C Reference

One of the ways writers link the different parts of a passage is by the use of words like *this*, *that*, to refer to things or facts that have gone before. Look through the text to see what the following refer to:

1 line 1   *they* refers to . . . *The reason* . . . refers to . . .
2 line 18   *this* refers to the statement that . . .
3 line 27   *these* refers to . . .
4 line 45   *this* refers to . . .
5 lines 46–51   *Doctors who . . . accidents at work* refers back to . . .

Overall understanding

1 What do you think would be the best title for the passage?
  (a) How accidents are caused
  (b) Human factors in accidents
  (c) How to prevent accidents on the roads and in factories
  (d) Accidents and anxiety
  Explain your choice.

2 Complete this sentence which is a summary of the passage: *Accidents are not just caused by chance or by physical factors; in fact, very often . . . for example . . .*

3 Is any of the information in the passage of use to you in writing your report? If so, what notes would you take from it?

Using your reading

1 If you wanted to use the information in this passage in your report what title would you put it under?
2 What conclusion could you draw from this information about the possibility of completely eliminating accidents from the factory?
3 Are there any practical steps which could be taken – as a result of what is in the passage – to reduce the number of accidents caused by human factors? Does it have any relevance to selection of workers and the make-up of work teams? To the decision on work rate? To the style of authority in the factory?

One member of the group or class should present what is in the passage: the factors which cause accidents. Others should suggest the consequences of these factors. *This means we should . . .*
Write down the conclusion to the discussion in the form of *Recommendations*.

Summary

In this unit you have worked on:
– reference
– the implications or consequences of what you read.
– applying the *general* meaning to a particular situation.

5 What constitutes a race?

Situation

Gabriel Okpaye came to study in England four or five months ago; although he is settling down quite well in England and enjoying his course of studies he was upset a few days ago when one of his fellow-students remarked in a discussion – 'Of course Africans have a completely different mentality and outlook from Europeans; I'm not a racist but there are differences between peoples'.

Gabriel knew that he didn't agree with this idea, but found it very difficult to argue effectively because he had no specific information or knowledge about racial differences; in the college library he discovered a book – *The Fundamentals of Psychology* with a chapter on *Race and Sex Differences* . . .

Think it over

Try to define what you mean by *race*; give some examples of places where there is a lot of racial prejudice – why do you think some countries have made distinction between races part of their system?

Can you make suggestions for eliminating racial injustice? Are there any laws in your country which try to prevent racial prejudice?

In what ways is racial prejudice often expressed?

WHAT DO YOU KNOW ALREADY?

WHAT IS HIS READING PURPOSE?

How will he approach his reading?
– skimming?
– scanning?
– close reading?
Do you think he should take notes?

Text

Use the reading strategy which you have decided would be most appropriate for Gabriel Okpaye.

What Constitutes a Race?

For the layman the answer to this is easy. There are five races; white, yellow, red, black and brown. It is just a matter of colour. But there are some negroes who are lighter in colour than some of the so-called whites, and we are not talking about half-castes here. Europeans who live in hot countries acquire brown skins, and even sunbathing enthusiasts in Europe acquire a tan.

When we think about it, we are inclined to think that we are concerned with more than the colour of the skin and begin to mention differences in hair and eye colour, shape of nose, length of limbs etc. And even when we examine all of these it is not easy to make a firm classification: there are three main forms of hair – straight, curly and woolly. In colour it may be blond, brunette or red. On this criterion Australian blacks would be grouped with Europeans. Hair colour would distinguish different types of Europeans, but the rest of the world would be in the same group of brunettes. Eye colour, which is inherited, is too varied to give good classification.

So we see that it is very difficult to define race, which means that the results of tests which claim to prove that one race is superior to another must be regarded with suspicion. There *are* some tests which are fairly reliable and from them we can draw some tentative conclusions: there is no strong evidence that any race is superior in any respect. For example, it has frequently been said that 'primitive' peoples have a better sense discrimination than people living in urban communities, but there is no proven evidence of this. Any difference is probably due more to familiarity with the environment than racial differences; the marvellous ability of the Australian hunter is paralleled by the doctor's work with a stethoscope. As far as intelligence is concerned, the tests we do have suggest that racial differences do not exist where fair tests are used. Even if one group may seem inferior to another it is usually a question of knowledge, not of ability – with practice the different groups reach very similar average levels.

From *The Fundamentals of Psychology*, by C. J. Adcock, published by Methuen & Co. Ltd.

WHAT KIND OF TEXT?

What kind of text do you think this is? Is it written by an expert or by a journalist or populariser?
Does it come from a book, a magazine or a newspaper?
Is it written for experts or the general public?

Language work

A Degrees of certainty

The passage is written by a scientist and because he wants to be precise and exact he is careful to indicate whether what he says is certain, probable, or only possible; here are some of the expressions which indicate the degree of certainty.

If you say *there are no essential differences between racial types* you are presenting this as something you consider *certain*. If you say *there may be differences in behaviour due to different living conditions* the use of *may* indicates that you are not certain of what you want to suggest but you think it is possible. .

When you want to write very accurately you try to indicate how certain you are of what you write, so you use words like *fairly, rather, possibly, probably, seem, suggest, tentative, likely*.

possible		certain
possibly	probably	surely certainly
seem } suggest }		is will
might } may }		
fairly } rather } + adj quite }		very extremely

What do you think is the difference between *I think* and *I am inclined to think?*

Fill in a table like the one below with the following expressions:

Europeans who live in hot climates acquire brown skins (lines 4–5)
we are inclined to think that we are concerned with more than colour (lines 7–8)
it is not easy to make a firm classification (line 10)
In colour it may be blond, brunette or red. (lines 11–12)
There are some tests which are fairly reliable (lines 19–20)
we can draw some tentative conclusions (line 20)
Any difference is probably due more to familiarity (lines 24–5)
the tests we do suggest that . . . (lines 27–8)
Even if one group may seem inferior to another . . . (lines 28–9)

Possible	Probable	Certain

B Vocabulary

1 *Classification* (line 10) involves dividing things or ideas into different . . .
2 A *criterion* (line 12) is a standard or rule by which something can be . . .
3 If we regard the results of tests with *suspicion* (line 19) does that mean we can believe these results or not?
4 *Sense discrimination* (lines 22–3) means the ability to identify differences by means of the senses like hearing . . . and . . .

C Reference

1 What does *this* in line 1 refer to?
2 *It* in line 2 refers to . . .
3 What are *these* in line 10?
4 *Which* in line 17 refers to . . .
5 What does *this* in line 24 refer to?
6 *Similar* in line 31 compares . . .

D Comprehension

Paragraph 1

1 What does the title indicate you will learn from the passage?
2 What is the layman's definition of race? Is it correct?
   Therefore a 'layman' is someone who . . .
   What would you consider to be the opposite of 'layman'?

Paragraph 2

3 Complete this summary of the paragraph:
   Many kinds of . . . have been suggested as ways of differentiating . . . for example, hair colour, the shape of the nose . . . but these are not very useful because . . .
4 Is the point about eye colour (a) an additional point about the main topic of the paragraph, or (b) a new piece of information changing what has just been said?

Paragraph 3

5 Does the use of *so* as first word indicate that the paragraph is (a) a consequence (b) a cause (c) a change in what has been said previously?

6 Explain the following:
   a) There *are* some tests which are fairly reliable (lines 19–20). Why is 'are' italicised?
   b) The tests we *do* have suggested . . . Why does the writer say 'do have' instead of just 'have'?
   c) ' . . . in the morning, but I *do* like coffee.' Suggest a suitable start to the sentence.
       Finish the sentences:
   d) 'I very rarely go to the theatre, but . . .'
   e) 'I can't play tennis very well, but . . . '
   f) ' . . . , but I *have* got a bike.'
7 In lines 25–6 the writer gives an example about *primitive people*. What is it an example of? The fact that . . .
8 'it has frequently been said that . . . ' Does this expression mean that what follows is (a) likely, (b) unlikely to be true?
9 ' . . . is paralleled by . . . ' implies that the Australian hunter is good at . . . and the doctor good at . . . Each is equally good in his own . . .

Overall understanding

1 What points could Gabriel Okpaye draw from this text which would allow him to defend effectively his point that racial differences are not important?
2 Would he be justified in saying experiments have proved there is no difference in intelligence between people of different races?
3 Could he say it has been shown that primitive peoples have a better sense of touch and smell than Europeans?
4 Would he be right if he said Europeans who go and live in hot climates lose their racial characteristics?
5 In the text we see that people often hold opinions that experts consider to be mistaken. Find two opinions of this kind in the passage.
6 What is the basic conclusion of the text about (a) what constitutes a race, (b) the differences between people of different races?

Using your reading

1   Gabriel Okpaye chose *Introduction to Psychology* as one of his optional study courses – one of the study topics was *Race differences and racial prejudice*. He was asked to find information about a number of points and to prepare notes to give a short talk on this in class. Fill in any information in the reading text which might be of use to him for this:

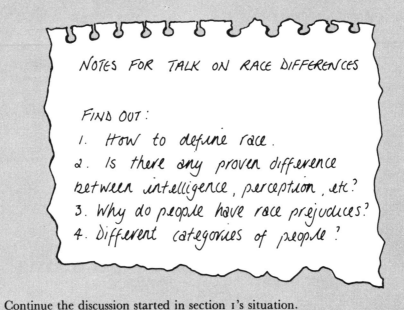

NOTES FOR TALK ON RACE DIFFERENCES

FIND OUT:
1. How to define race.
2. Is there any proven difference between intelligence, perception, etc?
3. Why do people have race prejudices?
4. Different categories of people?

2   Continue the discussion started in section 1's situation.

Summary

In this unit you have worked on:
- picking out useful information for an argument;
- identifying degrees of certainty;
- generalisations and examples.

You have seen the kind of language used to describe facts and experiments.

6 How the smallpox war was won

Situation

Transmalia is a small country in West Africa – in the rainy part where there is dense tropical forest. One of the country's main problems is in the north of the country where yellow fever is endemic and in most villages there are a number of cases each year. The problem of controlling the disease is made difficult by the fact that many of the people who live in the north are nomads who wander across the borders of neighbouring countries, which makes it almost impossible to check on the whole population.

You are a Transmalian, just back from Europe and have been appointed to a job in the Ministry of Health. You have been instructed to prepare a report on the *methods* that could be used to eradicate* yellow fever from your country. One weekend at home you saw an article entitled *How the Smallpox war was won* . . .

WHAT IS YOUR READING PURPOSE? DO YOU WANT TO KNOW DETAILS OR A GENERAL APPROACH?

Yellow fever: an acute disease of certain tropical localities, characterised by fever and jaundice.*
Causes: the disease is due to a virus which is transmitted to man by the Aedes Aegypti mosquito.
Monkeys are an important reservoir of infection where the disease is endemic.* The virus is found in the blood of infected individuals during the first three or four days of the disease.
Epidemics take place during the hot season and it is much more dangerous for a susceptible person to visit some centre of yellow fever during the hot months than during the cooler ones.
Preventive treatment is important, and consists of vaccination of everyone travelling to and from those parts of the world where the disease occurs. The sick must be kept for the first three days of illness in rooms protected by mosquito netting, so that they may not infect mosquitoes which would pass the disease to healthy individuals.
The same general measures as in the case of malaria should be taken against mosquitoes.

Yellow lotion: a lotion prepared from mercury bichloride 3 gm, boiling distilled water 35 cc, calcium hydroxide solution of sufficient quantity to make 100 ... ...l and stimulant. It is used f...

Do you think the definition of yellow fever comes from: (a) a dictionary? (b) a popular book about medicine? (c) a medical dictionary?

Footnote: * If you cannot guess the meaning of these words from the context, check in a dictionary.

Think it over

What is your purpose – in your position in the Ministry of Health – in reading about the campaign against smallpox? What kind of information will be useful to you? What kind of information, in an article about smallpox in East Africa is *not* relevant to your purpose.

In your task of finding a method to eradicate yellow fever, it would probably be useful to make a list of the problems to be solved. If you have these in mind while you are reading you can check if the text can be applied to any of them.

WHAT DO YOU KNOW ALREADY?

Text

Read the passage with reference to the checklist of problems you have prepared. Note those for which there is information which may be useful to you.

CHECKLIST.
Pbs. to be solved in yellow
fever campaign.
1. How to locate all those who
have the disease.
2.
3.
4.
5.

If no more cases of smallpox are reported by the end of the year the World Health Organisation can declare the world free of this deadly disease.

The world's last known case of smallpox (outside an outbreak in a Birmingham laboratory) was reported in Somalia, in the Horn of Africa, in October 1977. The victim was a young cook called Ali Maow Maalin. His case becomes a landmark in medical history – for smallpox is the first communicable disease ever to be eradicated.

The remarkable campaign to free the world from smallpox has been led by the World Health Organisation. The Horn of Africa, embracing the Ogaden region of Ethiopia and Somalia was one of the last smallpox-ridden areas of the world when the WHO-sponsored Smallpox Eradication Programme (SEP) got under way in 1971.

Many of the twenty-five million inhabitants, mostly farmers and nomads living in a wilderness of desert, bush and mountains, already had smallpox. The problem of tracing the disease in such formidable country was made even more difficult by the continuous warfare in the country.

The programme concentrated on an imaginative policy of 'search and containment'. Vaccination was used to reduce the widespread incidence of the disease; but the success of the campaign depended on the work of volunteers. These were men, paid by the day, who walked hundreds of miles in search of 'rumours' – information about possible smallpox cases. Often these rumours turned out to be cases of measles chicken pox or syphilis – but nothing could be left to chance. As the campaign progressed the disease was gradually brought under control. By September 1976 the SEP made its first report that no new cases had been reported.

But that first optimism was short-lived. A three-year old girl called Amina Salat, from a dusty village in the Ogaden in the south-east of Ethiopia, had given smallpox to a young nomad visitor. Leaving the village, he had walked across the border into Somalia. There he infected 3000 people, and among them had been the cook Ali. It was a further fourteen months before the elusive target zero was reached. Even now the search continues in 'high risk' areas and in parts of the country unchecked for some time. The flow of rumours has now diminished to a trickle – but each must still be checked by a qualified person.

Victory is in sight, but two years must pass since the 'last case' before an international committee can declare that the world is entirely free from smallpox.

Abridged and adapted from an article by Marion Kaplan in the *Observer Colour Supplement*, 26.3.1979

Language work

A Vocabulary

Use what you can find from the context and the forms of words (see Unit 1) to work out the meanings of:

1 *eradicated* (line 10) – will there *still* be people who have smallpox?
2 *communicable* (lines 8–9) – able to be . . .
3 *smallpox-ridden* (lines 16–17) –
4 these rumours *turned out* to be . . .
5 an *elusive* target – was it easy to find?
6 diminished to *a trickle* – is this a great or very small quantity?

B Reference

His case becomes a *landmark* in medical history – for smallpox is the first communicable disease ever to be *eradicated*. (lines 6–10)

The *remarkable* campaign to *free the world* from smallpox had been led by the World Health Organisation. (lines 11–13)

In explanatory texts like the one in this unit it is important to understand the way in which the various parts of the text are related. In the two sentences given here the relationship is made by repeating in the second sentence part of the meaning of the first. Sentence 1 says that the case of Ali is a *landmark*, something to be noticed or *remarked*, and the same idea is taken up in sentence 2 with the word *remarkable*. In the same way, the idea of *eradicate* is repeated in *to free the world from smallpox*.

See if you can find how the links are made in these sentences:

1(a) Many of the twenty-five million inhabitants, mostly farmers and nomads, living in a wilderness of desert, bush and mountains, already had smallpox. (lines 21–5)
 (b) The problem of tracing the disease in such formidable country was made even more difficult by the continuous warfare in the country. (lines 25–8)

Such formidable country refers to . . .

2(a) The programme concentrated on an imaginative policy of search and containment.
 (b) Vaccination was used to reduce the widespread incidence of the disease. (lines 31–3)
 (c) These were men, paid by the day, who walked hundreds of miles in search of 'rumours'. (lines 35–7)

Vaccination is an example of search? containment?
The men . . . who walked hundreds of miles is an example of search? containment?

3(a) By September 1976 the SEP made its first report that no new cases had been reported. (lines 44–6)
 (b) But that first optimism was shortlived . . . (lines 47–8)

That first optimism in sentence 3(b) refers back to . . .

C Comprehension

Your purpose in reading this is to see if it gives you any ideas on 'methods of organising a campaign against an infectious disease in a tropical country'. Go through paragraph by paragraph marking if there is anything relevant to your purpose:

Paragraph 1
Relevant   Irrelevant
What?   Why? only information about . . .

You should follow the same method for the remaining paragraphs.

Overall understanding

1 What is the general importance of the events described in the text?
   It is the first time . . .
2 What were the main difficulties involved in eliminating smallpox from Ethiopia and Somalia?
   (a) . . .
   (b) . . .
   (c) . . .
3 The policy adopted was one of 'search and containment'. What did this mean in practice?
   In the *search* part of the campaign, volunteers . . .
   Containment involved a programme of systematic . . .
4 What setback happened when it seemed that the war against smallpox had been successful?
5 In what month of what year did they finally reach a point where there were no cases of smallpox?
6 Is it sure that smallpox has been eradicated?
7 What work is going on at the time when the article was written?
8 How much of the information in your answers to the questions is applicable to the yellow fever situation in Transmalia?

Using your reading

Use the information you have about the methods used in Somalia and Ethiopia – and your own solutions to the problems involved – to plan the campaign against yellow fever in Transmalia. Present it in the form of a report like this:

```
Problems                        Solutions

1 How to locate every person    1 Use volunteers to trace
  suffering from disease           rumours.

2                               2

3                               3
```

Summary

In this unit you have worked on picking out relevant from irrelevant information; in applying this information to a practical problem. You have examined some ways in which different parts of a text are connected.

7 Hitchhiking

Situation

Three students, Johan, Anne-Marie and Kate, are coming to the end of their year's stay in England and have decided to spend their summer holidays together. They plan to spend two weeks in Rome, Florence and Venice, and then to travel along the coast of Yugoslavia until they find a small village with a good beach. The trouble is that – like most students – they are short of money and want to arrange their holiday as economically as possible.

Johan is very keen on hitchhiking:

'We wouldn't spend a penny on transport – it'd be more comfortable than going by train or bus – and we'd meet all sorts of interesting people on the road.'

Anne-Marie and Kate are more reticent:

'Hitchhiking can be risky – I've heard about several incidents where girls especially have been attacked. And you can never be sure when you're going to get a lift or where you'll have reached by the end of the day'.

'And in any case I don't like asking for something without paying. Even if it costs more I prefer to go by train.'

'In that case it means we'll only be able to afford two weeks' holiday instead of a month. – have you seen how high train fares are?'

But Johan couldn't convince his friends that hitchhiking would be best, then one day he saw a newspaper article . . .

WHAT IS JOHAN'S PURPOSE IN READING?

Is he interested in all the details of the text?
Does he want to know about the writer's attitude to the problem?
Will he read closely or scan?
Do you think he will want to take any notes?

Think it over

What are your opinions about hitchhiking? Do you approve or disapprove of it?
What are the advantages and disadvantages of hitchhiking as a form of travel?
Can hitchhiking be considered a way of solving traffic congestion?

WHAT DO YOU KNOW ALREADY?

Text

Institutionalising the Belgian Hitchhiker

by Gary Yerkey

In 1947 Jack Kerouac wrote '*On the Road*' about his experiences as a hitchhiker and in doing so enriched the meaning of hitchhiking – to beg free rides in passing motor-vehicles – for a generation to come. The 'greatest' ride in his life came one day in Minnesota when 'a truck driven by two young farmers – the most smiling, cheerful couple of handsome bumpkins you could ever wish to see – were picking up everyone who wanted a ride, with broad howareyou smiles. I ran up and said, "Is there room?" They said, "Sure, hop on, 'sroom for everybody."'

Now comes Taxistop, an organisation founded in Brussels several months ago whose aim is no less than the institutionalising of hitchhiking itself. It says, ''sroom for everybody still but now it's going to cost.'

The idea makes sense, perhaps too much, and its intentions are noble. Drivers and hitchhikers both pay 200 Belgian francs (about $ 6.75) to join Taxistop. For the fee they receive a handsome plaque inscribed with the *Taxistop* and the organisation's logo. Drivers display it in their windshields. Hitchhikers hold it up instead of thumbs. When they meet each other on the road, the former stops to pick up the latter, assured by the screened membership that the new passenger (probably) won't hit him over the head. When the hitchhiker disembarks he pays the driver 1 Belgian franc (about 3 cents) for each kilometer travelled, with a reduction of 50 centimes for every kilometer beyond 100.

'Yes', conceded Guy Baysn, 43, an ecologist and Vice-President of Taxistop. 'We have encountered some opposition to the idea – from people who argue that hitchhiking shouldn't be institutionalised, also from those who find the idea encourages the use of the automobile.'

But his reply to critics is that Taxistop is the only solution to the double-edged problem of, on the one hand, an inadequate system of public transport and, on the other, wasteful use of a necessary evil, the automobile.

Taxistop now has 1,500 drivers and hitchhikers as members. It has issued an eight-Point Code of Honour for its members to use as a guide for behaviour. 'Always have small change available,' Point 4 counsels the hitchhiker. 'Do not smoke without first obtaining the permission of the driver,' Point 6 warns. And Point 5, apparently to be followed up in the event of meeting a grumpy driver, cautions; 'Do not force conversation against the driver's will'. So endeth the Beat Generation.

WHAT KIND OF TEXT?

This is taken from a newspaper. Is it news or comment? Mainly facts or opinions?

Abridged and adapted from the article *Institutionalising the Belgian Hitchhiker* by Gary Yerkey, in the *International Herald Tribune*, 15.4.1979.

Language work

A Vocabulary and reference

1 lines 3–4 *in doing so* – what does *so* refer to?

2 line 13 *bumpkins* – guess from the context what this is likely to mean.
Someone who . . .

3 line 16–17 *broad howareyou smiles* – what idea does *howareyou* give?

4 line 19 *'sroom for everybody* – *'sroom* is an abbreviated form of . . .
Why is it written like this?

5 lines 23–4 *immunising* is a suffix which means making something immune.
Institutionalising means . . .

6 What would be the opposite of the idea expressed by *institutionalised* here?
a) Unorganised b) Legalised c) Not allowed.

7 lines 27–8 *perhaps too much* – Is this (a) information about Taxistop? (b) a comment by the author? What comment or information is given?

8 line 35 *logo* – look at the illustration to find out what *logo* means . . .

9 lines 40–2 *the former* refers to . . . *the latter* refers to . . . *screened membership* – this means that members are . . . before joining to make sure that . . .

10 lines 45–50 *Paris to Rome is 960 kilometers* – how much would it cost with Taxistop if you got three lifts of equal distance?

11 lines 58–60 *those who think the idea encourages the use of the automobile.*
Does the sentence refer to people who are (a) in favour of increased use of cars? (b) people who oppose this?

12 line 61 *critics* – this refers to . . .

13 line 63 *the double-edged problem* – why is the problem referred to as double-edged? What are the two aspects of the problem? How does Taxistop help to solve them?

14 lines 64–6 Notice the use of *on the one hand* and *on the other* in an explanation of opposites, or of two aspects of a question.

15 lines 66–7 *a necessary evil* – (a) suggests that the use of cars should be encouraged, (b) states that cars should be condemned as being evil, (c) considers that there is no alternative to the use of cars.

16 lines 73–9 There are three words here with the meaning *give advice* especially about things to be avoided. What are they?

17 line 81 *grumpy driver* – use the context to guess the meaning of grumpy.

18 line 84 *So endeth* – in what kind of writing in English will you find *-eth* as the ending of the third person singular instead of *'-s*? Is it likely to be modern or old? Why do you think it is used here?

19 line 84 What does *so* refer to here?

B Comprehension

Paragraph 1
The text tells you some facts about an organisation: it also gives you the writer's attitude to these facts. His attitude is illustrated by using a quotation from another writer.

The reading exercise will help you to see how attitudes can be expressed and how punctuation marks like quotation marks ' . . . ' show where a writer refers to other books or writers.

1 Who was Jack Kerouac? If you don't know, where would you look to find out?

2 *'On the Road'* – the ' . . . ' indicate that this is . . .

3 *to beg free rides from passing vehicles* – this is a quotation from?

4 Where does the quotation *a truck . . . 's room for everyone* come from?

5 What impression of hitchhiking is given in lines 5–7? That it is an activity in which people . . .

Paragraph 2
6 *Now comes Taxistop* – is what follows (a) a continuation of the ideas and impressions in lines 5–7, or (b) in contrast to them?

7 What is implied in the paragraph? In Kerouac's book, hitchhiking is presented as being . . . With the establishment of Taxistop it has become . . .

Paragraph 3
8 Here we have details of the way Taxistop functions:
(a) Who can join?
(b) What is the fee for joining?
(c) What do you get in return for the fee?
(d) How do members signal that they want a lift?

(e)	What do ordinary hitchhikers do to show they want one?

(f)	How much does a trip cost Taxistop members?

(g)	Are drivers sure they won't be hit over the head? Yes . . . No . . . Practically . . .

Paragraph 4

9	What are two objections to the Taxistop system mentioned?

10	What are Mr Baysn's replies to the objections?

11	Does the text give you any idea of Mr Baysn's reasons for taking a leading part in Taxistop?

Paragraph 5

12	What is the purpose of the Code of Honour?

13	Why should hitchhikers always have small change?

14	Why should they not smoke?

15	What does the *Beat Generation* refer to?

16	Is the last line (a) the writer's comment on Taxistop; (b) the final point in the description of the system; (c) a sign that this is the end of the article?

Overall understanding

1	What information could Johan get from the article which would be useful in his argument about whether to go hitchhiking or not?

2	Does the article give the author's attitude towards Taxistop? Do you think he is (a) favourable, (b) unfavourable, (c) without opinion about the organisation? Explain your answer.

3	Is the main topic of the text (a) hitchhiking in general, (b) Jack Kerouac, (c) Taxistop?
Do you think the writer of the text is (a) Belgian, (b) British, (c) American?

Using your reading

Continue the argument between Johan, Anne-Marie and Kate about whether to hitchhike on their holiday. You should use the description of Taxistop's activities to persuade the two girls; they should find all the possible objections to hitchhiking and the successful working of the scheme.

and/or
Use a description of Taxistop in a letter from Johan to Kate where he tries to convince her that it would be a good idea to join the organisation and hitchhike to Rome using its services.

Summary

You have used your reading to provide you with ideas and information to use in an argument; you have thought about how a writer can suggest his opinion on a question without actually stating it; you have interpreted the attitude of the writer as well as getting the practical details clear.

8 Censorship

Situation

Imagine you live in a society where there is at present a debate about the necessity for censorship of television – it is a topical question in most countries at most times – and you are interested in working out for yourself a clear opinion on this matter. Therefore your attention is attracted by the lines *The Case for Censoring Television Violence* . . .

WHAT IS YOUR READING PURPOSE?

Will you be more concerned with opinions or facts? Will you read quickly or carefully?

Think it over

When you read a controversial article you usually compare it with your own opinion and prejudices. What are your ideas about censorship in general? Do you think it is always wrong? Or always necessary? Do you think people are corrupted by seeing scenes of violence or sex, or do you believe everyone should be free to decide for himself what he watches or doesn't watch? What about children and TV? Have you got prejudices about these questions, or do you know any facts? What kind of questions would you want answers to, before deciding on your opinion (or changing it)?

WHAT OPINIONS DO YOU BRING TO YOUR READING?

Text

The case for censoring television violence

by Conor Cruise O'Brien

Broadcasters are against censorship. That much was clear at a recent symposium on the subject of censorship at the Edinburgh International Television Festival.

It was not clear, however, what exactly broadcasters meant by censorship, or what a censor-free condition would be like. Some spoke as if they regarded the editing of anyone's work by anyone else as censorship. Others indicated that to refrain from saying or writing something others might object to is a form of self-censorship: it was implied that self-censorship was always a response to pressure from above – never to fashion or a desire for approval.

Because they are against censorship, one would expect broadcasters to be especially vigilant about the danger of commercial exploitation of socially harmful forces, such as the appeal of violence. But there are few signs of this – instead there are signs of a determination to play down serious evidence tending to show, for example, that exposure of children to television violence is likely to have a brutalising effect.

Evidence of this is provided in a recent book by H. S. Eysenck and D. K. B. Nias, *Sex, Violence and the Media*, which refers to the use of films by the American army to reduce the viewers' reaction to pain and suffering in others, so that in the end they will inflict pain and death without question.

The authors go on to set out in Chapter 7, Laboratory experiments showing that exposure to 'ordinary' or commercial televised violence can have a similar effect. With remarkable consistency, the groups of children and adults exposed to broadcast violence behaved more aggressively than the control groups.

Abridged and adapted from the article *The case for censoring television violence*, by Conor Cruise O'Brien, in *The Observer*, 28.10.78.

Language work

A Vocabulary

1   Notice the different ways of expressing the idea *x thinks*:

Lines 5–6   *Some spoke as if they regarded . . .*
Line 7   *Others indicated . . .*
Line 9   *it was implied that . . .*
What is the exact meaning of *implied*? Did the broadcasters *say* they thought that all self-censorship came from above?

2   Guess the meaning from the context.
Does *play down* (line 16) mean: (a) to make it seem important? (b) to make it seem unimportant?

3   *exposure of children to television violence is likely to have a brutalising effect* lines 17–18
Something which has a *tranquillising* effect makes people tranquil or calm: something which has a *brutalising* effect makes people . . . or . . .

4   *they regarded the editing of anyone's work by anyone else as censorship* lines 6–7
Does the context indicate that *editing* means (a) publishing/making known? (b) cutting/changing?

5   *With remarkable consistency*, lines 26–7
Consistency indicates that, (a) some groups behaved more ·violently, (b) all groups behaved more violently, (c) almost all groups behaved more violently!
Remarkable indicates that, (a) the results were surprising! (b) the results were as expected?

B Reference

Lines 1–2   *That much was clear at a recent symposium on the subject . . .* What does *that much* refer to?
This passage links ideas in a logical way. One of the ways of linking ideas is through using words like *this, that, so, similar* to refer to things or ideas that have been previously in the text.
For example in line 1 – *Broadcasters are against censorship. That much was clear at a . . .*
That much refers to the whole sentence that goes before. Can you identify what the following refer to?

Lines 5–7   *Some spoke as if they regarded . . . Others indicated that . . .*
Lines 14–15   *such as the appeal of violence*
Line 15   *But there are few signs of this*
Line 19   *Evidence of this is provided in a recent book . . .*
Lines 25–6   *commercial televised violence can have a similar effect . . .*

C Comprehension

Does the headline suggest that the writer is (a) in favour of censoring violence on TV? (b) against censoring violence on TV?
What does the word *Outlook* suggest? – that the text will contain news and information, or opinions?

Paragraph 1 What is the context of the article? The author is commenting on a recent . . . in which broadcaster declared that . . .

Paragraph 2 Does the word *however* indicate that the paragraph will (a) agree with or (b) modify or change the statement in paragraph 1? The paragraph points out a *contrast* in the opinions of the broadcasters about censorship.
What is this contrast?
What words are used to show this?

Paragraph 3 This contains a statement one would expect and a contradiction of this statement – *but*.
What are the two points?

Paragraph 4 This gives a description of one experiment giving evidence of the writer's main point. Put these in simple terms.
The US Army used films of violence to . . .
This is evidence of the point that . . .
There is a second experiment described. Fill in the details of the schemes:
Groups of children and adults were shown . . .
Control groups did not . . .
The behaviour of the control groups was . . .

Overall understanding

1 Why does the writer thinks there is a case for censoring violence on TV?

2 What does the writer say about the attitude of broadcasters to censorship? What does he say about their attitude to evidence that TV violence can cause violent behaviour?

3 Divide the passage into the facts included and the opinions expressed.

4 Which part of the article do you agree with? Which do you disagree with? Has the article changed or confirmed the opinions you had before reading it? Or has it had no effect?

Using your reading

The text is argumentative – it wants to convince people that what it says is true. When you take part in an argument you want to convince people, too, and a newspaper argument is open to readers. If you agree with the writer, write a letter to the editor beginning:

```
Dear Sir,
I cannot agree with Dr Conor Cruise O'Brien about the
need for TV censorship.  I think he is wrong for the
following reasons:
```

If you disagree with this case, you would begin:

```
Dear Sir,
I am writing to say how fully I support Dr Conor Cruise
O'Brien's article about censorship.  I would like to add
that ...
```

If you agree that some censorship is necessary, would you apply it to the following situations on TV: (a) a cowboy film? (b) a ganster film? (c) news film of violence? (d) news film of torture? (e) violence in cartoons?

Would you censor other things than violence on TV? If you disagree with censorship, what arguments would you give for allowing the above on television? Are there no restrictions you would make?

Summary

In this unit you have worked on the way in which writers develop arguments and the way in which they often *balance* them by stating an opinion and then bringing evidence to contradict this opinion.

You have also worked on the use of reference to provide links between different parts of a passage and on the way you can often guess from the context the meaning of an expression you do not know.

9 A problem of?

This unit differs from preceding ones. Instead of dealing with specific reading skills it asks you to use the kind of reading skills you have been practising to solve a problem and to interpret it. This will mean picking out the most important facts and judging the implications of them.

Text (a)

THE BLACK CYLINDER EXPERIMENT

Imagine a tall black cylinder standing on a white table in front of you. No one is near the table and there is nothing on the table except the cylinder which stands alone. Suddenly, without warning, the cylinder falls over with a crash. Why? No one has gone near it. Nothing has been seen to happen. There is no sound except the crash of the falling cylinder.

You are asked to try and understand what has happened and to write down your explanation on a card. But you have only ten minutes in which to think of an explanation – and you are not allowed to examine the cylinder in any way.

Understanding

1 Where do you think this problem is taken from? (a) a competition in a newspaper? (b) a physics textbook? (c) a book about psychology? (d) an intelligence test?
2 Explain your choice.
3 What are you asked to explain in the experiment? Why . . .
4 What are the *facts* described in the problem?
5 What can you see?
6 What happens?
7 What do you hear?
8 Why do you think it states very clearly: *No one is near the table and there is nothing on the table?*

Explanation

Without reading any further in the unit write *your* explanation of why the cylinder fell over. Do not take more than ten minutes to do this and do not talk to anyone about your explanation. Use a diagram to make your explanation if you want to.

The cylinder fell over because . . . . . .

If you are working in class each student can present his explanation and compare it with the other proposals.

Text (b)

Experimental subjects

The experiment was carried out on a number of different occasions. Altogether one thousand people took part. These people came from a wide variety of backgrounds, including university lecturers, research scientists, doctors, management executives, students and teachers.

Relevance

The black cylinder experiment was deliberately kept simple so that the thinking processes involved in trying to understand the phenomenon could be easily understood. What relevance does this experiment have to everyday thinking? There are the following points which are common to everyday thinking and to the black cylinder experiment.

1 Not enough information is given.
2 There is no opportunity to collect the data one needs.
3 Trial and error experimentation is not possible.
4 There is no way of checking whether an idea is right or wrong.
5 It is not a closed situation in which one can prove that one is right.
6 There may be several different explanations.
7 One is dealing with vague ideas and not with precise numbers which can be put through a mathematical formula.
8 In spite of the inadequate information one is required to come to a definite conclusion.
9 It is not so much a question of checking ideas, but of thinking of them first.
10 There is no one to ask.

Out of the thousand people who took part in the experiment, only three wrote on their cards *I do not care*. This is a perfectly valid response for no one is obliged to understand anything. If you do not care to understand something then you must borrow an explanation or do without one.

29

From *Practical Thinking*, by Edward de Bono, published by Jonathan Cape Ltd.

Understanding

1 Does the paragraph *Experimental subjects* help you to answer the question asked on page 38 – *Where do you think this problem is taken from?*

2 What do the different categories of people who took part in the experiment have in common? Are they representative of all classes of society?

3 *Relevance* means the quality of being connected to the subject. Read the sentence *The black cylinder . . . understood* at the beginning of the section on *Relevance*.

   Is the experiment connected to the subject of:
   (a) understanding the thinking processes?
   (b) understanding the phenomenon of the black cylinder falling?

4 What particular thinking processes are we concerned with here: (a) scientific explanation? (b) everyday thinking?

5 What is the general implication of the paragraph?
   The purpose of the black cylinder experiment is to examine how . . .

6 Ten points are given here. What are they examples of?
   Ways in which the black cylinder experiment is similar to . . .

7 Point 1 *not enough information is given* – what is it that we don't know? . . .

8 Point 2 *no possibility to collect data* – What data would you want to collect? How?

9 Point 3 *trial and error experimentation impossible* – What does *trial and error* mean?

10 Point 5 *experiment not a closed situation* – a closed situation is one in which there is a limited number of possibilities. Why is the experiment an open situation?

11 Point 7 *experiment doesn't deal with mathematical formulae and precise numbers* – What kind of experiments do deal with precise formulae and numbers? . . .

12 Point 8 *in spite of the inadequate information . . .* – rewrite this point beginning *Although . . .*

13 Point 9 *not so much a question of checking ideas, but of thinking of them first* – what does *them* refer to?

14 Do you agree that all the features mentioned in the list are similar to the situation in everyday thinking? If you do not agree which ones do you think are different?

Solutions

Here are some of the answers given by people who did the experiment:

Group one

```
     'It fell.
     'The black cylinder suddenly fell
over.'
     'It changed position suddenly.'
     'Fell over on its side.'
     'The tube fell over.'
     'Changed from a vertical to a
horizontal position.'
```

Suggested title: . . . .

Group two

```
     'With God all things are
possible.'
     'By magic.'
     'I don't understand it therefore
it is magic.'
     'Some magical process.
     'Mirrors? Weights and pulleys?
Magic!'

     'It fell over - reason gravity.'
     'Some clockwork or gravity device
in the black cylinder created an
imbalance after a period of time
causing it to topple.'
     'The black cylinder fell over
because an electrical charge
knocked it over.'
     'Due to an electrical current.'
     'Electrical impulse operating
from a battery made the black
tower topple.'
     'Electric magnet.'
     'Black thing received a jolt from
electric battery.'
     'Equilibrium inside changed due
to shocks.'
```

Suggested title: . . . .

Group three

```
     'Overbalanced due to a slow
shifting of contents.'
     'Change of balance due to rising
object in the tube.'
     'Because of its upright position
a weight inside it moved upwards and
made it overbalance.'
     'Something at the bottom rose up
to make it top-heavy...overbalanced.'
     'Cylinder fell due to becoming
top-heavy.'
```

Suggested title: . . . .

Group four

        'You kicked the desk.'
        'An accomplice hiding behind the
    desk knocked it over while we were
    preoccupied.'
        'Someone shot it down from the
    window on the right.'
        'Vibrations of overhead projector
    together with fans and breeze from
    window acting on a barely stable
    situation.'
        'The tube was unstable but was
    stuck to the table by adhesive
    which eventually gave way.'
        'Concealed clockwork mouse with
    suction pad feet climbs up tube
    which becomes top-heavy and falls
    over. Clockwork mechanism is
    silent.'

Suggested title: . . . .

Read each group of reasons and try to find a title which is common to each group. Discuss which reasons you find most satisfactory.

Here are the titles the writer gave to his four groups: (a) The Way it Works (b) Full details (c) Give it a Name (d) Simple Descriptions. Which title would you apply to each of the groups?

If you think it is useful for the discussion place the explanations you have given in the appropriate groups.

Diagrams

Here are four diagrams drawn by people who did the experiment:

Each diagram explains how the cylinder might have been caused to fall. Try to put into words the explanation given in each diagram.

Are the explanations possible? Which ones seem most satisfactory? Have you any objections to the explanations shown in the diagrams?

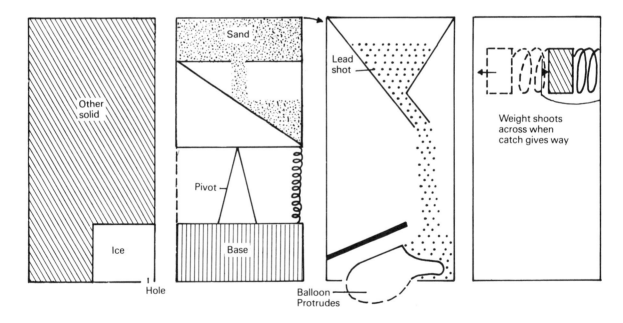

Illustrations by Alan Tunbridge, from *Practical Thinking*, by Edward de Bono, published by Jonathan Cape Ltd.

Overall understanding

What, if anything has the unit taught you about the way people solve problems? What title would you give to the unit?

Summary

This unit has given you practice in following instructions; in working out general implications from a number of details; in transforming diagrams into words.

10 Using and understanding charts

When you are reading for information you are likely to have to interpret diagrams and charts as well as to understand.

This unit contains exercises which require you to work out the meaning of charts, and the information you can obtain from them. The first three charts are what are called *pie charts*.

The circle represents the *total* of whatever you are concerned with – in chart one, people living in towns or suburbs.

The slices represent the proportion of the total. Five years ago about 16% of the population lived in the suburbs; 84% in urban areas – in towns.

Situation

You are the Sales Manager of a company which manufactures vacuum cleaners – it is part of your job to know a lot about the market for your product, about the performance of your company and its competitors and about the work of the salesmen in your department. Every day you receive a large number of reports . . . Here are some of the charts you receive on a typical day in the office.

Put into words the information that you can get from the three graphs:

Chart one tells you about . . .
Chart two indicates that . . .
From chart three it can be seen that . . .

Chart one

Population moves to the suburbs from town centres

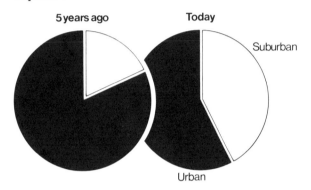

5 years ago   Today   Suburban   Urban

Chart two

Ages of the company's salesmen

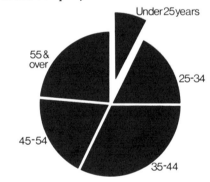

Under 25 years
55 & over
25-34
45-54
35-44

Chart three

The different activities in a salesman's day

Travelling   Recruiting new business
Open debt collection   Desk work
Office meeting

The information you get from charts will make you ask yourself questions. Which questions would you ask after studying the three charts above?

1 Should we reduce the number of salesmen in the centre of big towns?
2 Should we advertise for new salesmen with at least ten years' experience?
3 Should we cut down the number of forms salesmen have to fill in?

4 Should we send salesmen to visit housing estates on the outskirts of towns?
5 Should we recruit some younger salesmen?
6 Should we give a special bonus to salesmen who find new customers?

The three charts on page 42 are *pie charts* – they are useful for showing at a glance the proportions or percentages of expenses or activities.

Choosing what to emphasize

Here are four charts showing the movements of the company's sales over a period of years. Each is presented differently in order to put the emphasis on different features of the information.

What information do the charts give?
In which year were sales highest?
In which year were they lowest?

In which year was there no increase in sales?
In which year was there the smallest increase on the previous year's sales?
In which year was there the largest increase?
What is the general trend? Increasing? Steady? Falling?

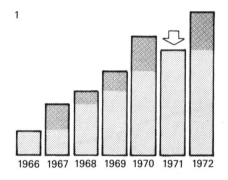

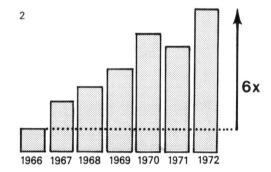

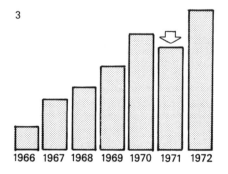

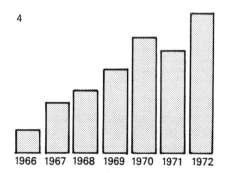

Here are the titles which were given to the charts, showing which piece of information is being emphasized. Connect the right title to the four charts:

A `Despite extended strike in 1971, 1972 company sales were at their highest level since 1966....`

B `Extended strike in 1971 temporarily slowed growth of company sales....`

C `Since 1964, company sales have risen in every year except one....`

D `Company sales in 1972 were six times their 1966 value....`

Title A goes with Chart . . .
Title B goes with Chart . . .
Title C goes with Chart . . .
Title D goes with Chart . . .

How could you present the chart if you wanted to emphasise that the general trend of sales was increasing?

Drawing conclusions

Here are four charts which describe a situation; what conclusions can we draw from them?

This chart represents the annual sales of different salesmen in the company.

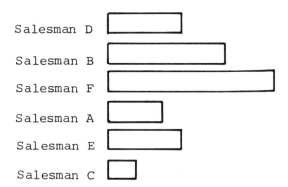

This chart shows the market for houses over a number of years. The black line shows the number of houses built; the dotted line shows the cost of building houses.

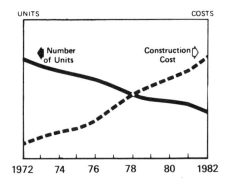

Which salesman has the highest sales? Which has the lowest?
What is the proportion of the highest to the lowest? The salesman with the highest sales sells . . . times more than the lowest.
Do you think it is natural that the difference between individual sales is so great? Suggest some reasons why there should be such a difference.

Complete the following sentence from the information contained in the graph:

In the last ten years the situation for people wanting to buy houses has become worse and worse, because . . .

If the trend on the graph continues in the same direction, will house prices rise further or begin to fall?

This chart shows the sales of a company over a period of years. In 1979 a new management team was appointed.

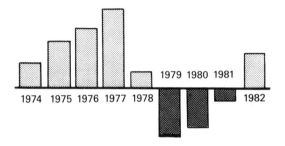

Has the appointment of a new management team been successful?
Describe the rises and falls in sales over the period covered in the chart:

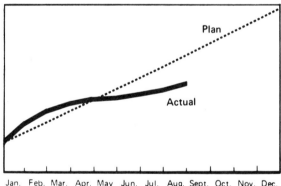

The dotted line shows the government forecast for economic growth during the year. The black line shows the growth that has in fact been achieved.
Were the government forecasts correct? Were they optimistic or pessimistic?
If the present trend continues, approximately what percentage difference will there be between the forecast and what happens?
What can you say about performance in the first four months of the year?

Charts by Gene Zelazny, from *Choosing and Using Charts*, by Gene Zelazny, published by Video Arts.

Summary

This unit has given you practice in understanding charts and graphs and in 'translating' the information you can find in them.

11 Young, broke and stuck at home

Situation

Jim Gregg is studying to be a teacher and is at present on a teacher training course in a college in London. The first topic of his course is called *Motivation* and for next week Jim has to give a talk on the needs and interests of the present-day teenager. He comes across the article *Young, Broke and stuck at home* in the college library . . .

WHAT IS YOUR READING PURPOSE?

Do you think Jim will look for facts, opinions, ideas, statistics? (choose as many of these as you think likely)
What does the title lead you to expect from the article?
– a scientific, sociological analysis of young people?
– an informal account of a young women's opinions?
– an objective account of the problems of living at home?
– an attack on present-day young people?
What reading approach will Jim use?
– scanning to see if there is anything relevant?
– skimming to get the main point of the article?
– reading closely to get every detail?
– relaxed reading for pleasure?
Do you think he will need to take notes?

Think it over

Use what you know about 15 and 16 year-olds to discuss the things they like about school; the things they don't like about school; the problems they are likely to have; their attitudes towards work/politics/their parents; the things they enjoy.
Pick out the adjectives which describe best what you think about today's teenagers:

hard-working	irresponsible	violent
lively	easy-going	lazy
political	uninterested	under-privileged
rich	well-educated	lucky
misunderstood	enthusiastic	tolerant
dirty	ungrateful	
well-dressed	scruffy	

Text

Read the text using the reading approach you decided would be most appropriate for Jim.

YOUNG, BROKE & STUCK AT HOME

In my family it's mainly Dad who enforces the rules – he always wants to know where I'm going, who with, and what time I'll be home. If I'm late, especially if I've been to a concert, he wants to know if there's been any trouble. He's less worried if I'm going to be with boys, because he thinks I'll be protected. In fact, there's usually more trouble when we've been out with boys than when we've been on our own. During the week I have to be at home by 10.30, which I think is reasonable. At weekends they don't mind too much, as long as I give them a rough idea of what time I'll be back. Some of my friends have to put up with much stricter rules. My best friend Julie's parents stop her going out if she's been late back even when she's got tickets for something. And a lot of my friends aren't allowed out on Sunday nights at all, which is quite a restriction since none of us can really go out a lot in the week, because of homework, especially now we've got exams.

My Dad's a teacher. I hate school and can't wait to get out of it, but this isn't a source of trouble between us. I've got a job fixed up for when I leave next term – if I was going on the dole, it might be a lot more difficult for us. I've hated school since the third year, when they started to say that if you don't get 'O' levels you won't get a job. I don't think 'O' levels count that much. It's mainly learning parrot fashion to show what a good memory you've got. I don't need them. I'm learning hairdressing. But I'm taking them anyway, so I can say to my teachers, 'See, I can do it!' I'll probably fail them all.

Like most young women living at home, I can't really talk about my ideas, or what I really feel, to my parents. It's difficult to have privacy at home. No-one ever knocks before they come into my room, and often I have to share it with my brother's girlfriend – it's just expected of me. I feel my parents are being nosy, even though they probably are not – so I don't talk to them about boys, or bring any back. Also I haven't talked all that much about what I think about racism and sexism. My Dad is against the National Front, but he doesn't really take sexism seriously. There are lots of examples of it in my house. Even though my mum does a full-time job, and nearly all the housework, she's not allowed a chequebook of her own. And my older brother makes stupid remarks about his girlfriend all the time, often just to irritate me. When my Dad knew I was writing this, he said, 'Tell them don't forget men's rights.' So I don't talk about these things, because they only get at me.

I didn't learn about racism or sexism at home or at school. Even though my school is mixed, none of the teachers have ever mentioned women's issues in any serious way. And even though it has many Black students, and even a few Black teachers, racism as such has never been discussed. Nor did anyone in my family ever mention it. I grew up feeling Black people were all criminals – because that's all you ever hear or read about. I didn't feel that I was either right or left wing – I'd never thought about it . . .

Young women like me don't have much money. What I do get I spend first on concerts, then on records. My parents give me money for clothes, and I have a Saturday morning hairdressing job, so I'm better off than many. That's another reason I hate school – all those rules and uniform when I could be at work earning. I know I won't get much at first, and I'll still have to live at home as it's so badly paid, but it'll be a start.

By Jan Phillips, *Spare Rib*, September 1980.

47

Where do you think the passage comes from? a) a book, b) a newspaper, c) a magazine?
Is it written for a special public or for everyone?
Do you get any impression of the political opinions expressed?

Language Work

A Formal and informal

The passage gives the impression that the person writes in the same way that she speaks, rather than in the rather different language used in more formal kinds of writing. This is done in three ways:

i)   using short forms of verbs (it's/I'll etc) rather than the full written forms (it is/I will). This imitates the way people speak.
Write the formal written form of these expressions from the passage:
He wants to know if *there's been* any trouble. (para 1)
He's less worried if *I'm going* to be with boys . . . (para 1)
I'd never thought about it . . . (para 5)

ii)   using informal words like *Mum and Dad* instead of the more formal *mother and father*.
If you put the first sentence of the text into reported speech you would say:
    She says that in her family it's mainly *her father who* . . .

iii)   Using one or two slang expressions. Try to guess what they mean from the context:
    Young, *broke* and stuck at home. (title)
    if I was going on *the dole* (para 2)
    I feel my parents are being *nosy* (para 3)

B Reference

What do the following refer to?

'My best friend Julie's parents stop her going out if she's been back late even if she's got tickets for *something*.' Here *something* refers to a . . . ?

'And a lot of my friends aren't allowed out on Sunday night at all, *which* is quite a restriction, since none of us can really go out a lot in the week.' *Which* refers to . . . ?
I'll probably fail them *all*. (end of para 3)
All refers to . . . ?

'When my Dad knew I was writing this, he said, "Tell *them* don't forget men's rights . . ."'
Who are *them?*

C Comprehension

There is a lot in the passage about Jane's attitudes and feelings, and the attitudes of her parents and friends. Scan the passage to find out:
– Her father's attitude to Jane's staying out late.
– His attitude to her going out with boys.
– Jane's attitude to the rules her father fixes about going out.
– Jane's attitude to school in general.
– Her attitude towards examinations.
– Her father's and brother's attitudes towards the women's movement.
– Jane's main leisure interests.
– Her attitude towards work.

D Implications

There are one or two references in the passage to things particularly connected with life in Britain – if you don't already know what they refer to, you can use the context to guess their meanings.
1   *O levels* (line 36) Why are these important in schools?
2   *National Front* (line 60) Is this concerned with racism, sexism or both? What does the title make it sound like?
3   *Concerts* (line 89) What kind of music do you think Jane goes to listen to?

Overall understanding

The passage tried to give a picture of the ideas and feelings of a typical teenage girl. If you have understood these you have understood the main points of your reading.
Discuss or write down the impression of Jane you get from the article. Use the questions to guide your idea:
– Is she happy or unhappy?
– Relations with parents?
– Likes and dislikes?
– Politically aware? What are her opinions?
– Ordinary or exceptional?
– How old do you think she is?

Using your reading

Jim Gregg uses some of the information as a basis for his talk on *The Needs and Interests of the Present-Day Teenager*. Below is the framework of his notes – what information from the passage would you use as examples for the talk?

1. Introduction: What teenagers like doing and what they dislike doing.

   Eg . . . .

2. Their need for independence.

   Eg . . . .

3. What they dislike in school.

   Eg . . . .

4. What they expect from school.

   Eg . . . .

Summary

In this unit you have practised reading fairly informal English, close to the way people speak: you have been interpreting the attitudes and feelings shown when people talk about themselves: you have had practice in scanning and using the context for interpreting specific references to Britain.

12 When a life depends on you

Situation

You're sitting on the beach and see someone drowning, driving on the motorway and see a crash, eating in a restaurant and see someone choking on his food. What do you do? The right prompt action can save the person's life.

Would you know what to do?

WHAT IS YOUR READING PURPOSE?

What will the reader expect to know at the end of reading the passage?

What kind of reading approach will be best?

Does the reader need to remember what he or she reads? How can he/she help make sure the important information is remembered?

Think it over

Can *you* answer the questions asked here? Write down what you would do if you faced the three situations – when you've read the passage check to see how far you would have been right.

WHEN A LIFE DEPENDS ON YOU

DROWNING

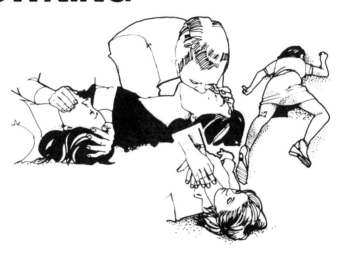

If you see someone drowning speed is vital. Once you get him out of the water, if he isn't breathing you have four minutes before his brain is irreparably damaged. Support the nape of his neck, tilt his head back and press his chin upwards. This stops the tongue blocking the airway in the throat and is sometimes enough to get him breathing again. If that doesn't work, start mouth to mouth breathing. Pinch his nostrils together with your fingers. Open your mouth wide and take a deep breath. Seal your lips around his mouth.

Blow into his lungs until his chest rises, then remove your mouth and watch his chest fall. Repeat twelve times a minute. Keep going until professional help arrives, but don't leave him to fetch it. Someone who has nearly drowned should always be taken to hospital.

To resuscitate a child — seal your lips around his mouth and nose and gently blow into his mouth. Give the first four breaths as quickly as possible to saturate the blood with oxygen. If, despite your efforts, he starts turning a blue-grey colour, you can feel no pulse and his pupils become dilated, heart massage is the last chance of saving his life. Put him on his back on a firm surface. Place yourself on one side. Feel for the lower half of the breastbone. Place the heel of your hand on this part of the bone with your palm and fingers off the chest. Cover this hand with the heel of the other hand. With arms straight, rock forwards pressing down on the lower half of the breastbone. For adults do 15 heart compressions followed by two lung inflations. For children up to ten, light pressure of one hand — about 60–80 times a minute — should be enough and do about 20 heart compressions. *Don't* be too violent or you may break a rib. Check how effective you are by seeing if his colour improves or his pulse becomes independent to your chest striking. If this happens stop the heart massage and place in the 'recovery position'. Otherwise continue until an ambulance arrives.

Do you think the passage comes from (a) a book, (b) a magazine?

Is it intended for the general public or medical specialists?

Language work

A Vocabulary

If the passage is to be of any practical use it is essential to understand it exactly. This requires knowing all the parts of the body referred to in the text. Use a dictionary to label the sketches of the body, head and hand shown.

The words are: *nape of neck: chin: tongue: throat: mouth: nostrils: lips: lungs: chest: pupils: breastbone: heel of hand: palm: fingers: rib.*

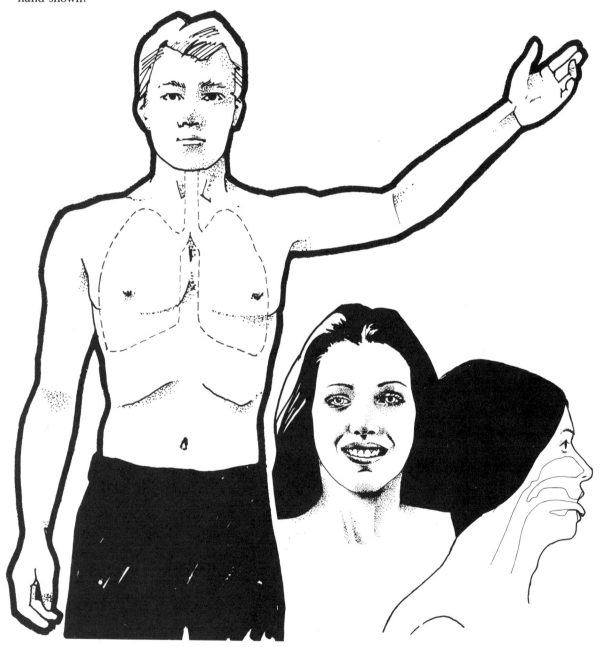

The passage also refers to a number of physical actions. These are written below together with their definitions. Match the words to their definitions:

1)	support	to cause to slope by raising one end
2)	tilt	to press between finger and thumb
3)	block	to bear the weight of something
4)	pinch	to become bigger or wider
5)	seal	to move regularly backwards and forwards
6)	blow	to search for something by touching
7)	dilate	to prevent anything from passing
8)	feel	to close completely
9)	rock	to send out air

Only definitions of the words with the meanings they have in the text are included here.

B Giving instructions

Notice that the text very often gives instructions in sentences beginning with *if*

If that doesn't work start mouth to mouth breathing.

If, despite your efforts, he starts turning a blue-grey colour, . . . , heart massage is the last chance of saving his life.

If this happens, stop the heart massage and place in the 'recovery position.'

The use of an *if* clause here is a way of telling someone when and under what conditions something should be done. Try to complete the following instructions:

If mouth to mouth doesn't work with a child . . .

If someone is drowning the first thing to do . . .

If the person's colour improves and his pulse becomes independent . . .

C Comprehension—understanding what to do

1 If you see someone drowning what do you do first? second? third?

2 Why is it so important to give first aid quickly?

3 What is the purpose of tilting the head back and pressing the chin upwards?

4 How long should you continue mouth to mouth breathing?

5 What would you do if you are trying to save a *child* from drowning?

6 Under what circumstances should you try heart massage?

7 How do you give heart massage?

8 What must you avoid when giving heart massage?

9 The instructions speak of 'lung inflation'. What is referred to here?

10 What symptoms tell you that the person you are saving has recovered?

Overall understanding

If you can answer the following questions adequately, you have understood the essential parts of the text:

What is the purpose of mouth to mouth breathing and heart massage?

When do I use each of these ways of reanimating people?

Do I know how to use the two methods?

What are the things I must *not* do if I have to save someone from drowning?

Use your reading

Write out a list of instructions for people to follow in an emergency.

WHAT TO DO IF YOU SEE SOMEONE DROWNING

1.

2.

3.

Further practice

The second part of the article was about road accidents. Work to get the same kind of exact understanding we got in the first text.

ROAD ACCIDENTS

Fire is one of the real dangers of a crash, so make sure the ignitions of all cars are turned off and don't let anyone smoke near the scene. Avoid pile-ups by stopping the traffic at least 200 metres away — preferably with a warning triangle or light. Get someone to telephone for an ambulance. Do not pull anyone injured out of a car or try to speed things up by rushing a victim to hospital yourself. Moving the injured is a job for the experts and you might make the damage worse. The exception is if there is danger of an explosion, when the casualty should be moved as gently as possible.

Any injured person will be suffering from shock — a killer in its own right — and anyone trapped in a car might panic. You can help by treating him for shock. Undo any tight clothing, cover him with a coat or blanket, but don't overheat him. Try to chat gently to take his mind off things.

Anyone wearing a seat belt when an accident happens might have a whiplash injury to the neck — a sign will be his chin right down on his chest. This makes breathing difficult and swallowing nearly impossible. So gently, with one hand on either side of his face, lift the chin upwards to clear the airway and make his breathing easier. Any heavy external bleeding must be stopped quickly. Grasp both sides of any wound and squeeze them together. Cover the area with a clean pad (an unused handkerchief will do). Lift the limb up and, as long as there is no fracture, press gently but firmly down on the wound.

If a pedestrian is knocked down, try not to move him. Treat for shock if he is conscious, give artificial respiration (see *Drowning*) if not.

By Angela Levin, from *The Observer Magazine*, July 9, 1978

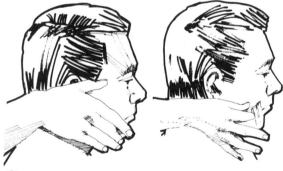

Summary

In this unit you have worked on understanding important instructions exactly; on building up areas of vocabulary (the body, movements) to help understand the text; on transforming this information to a short list of instructions.

You still don't know what to do if you see someone choking on his food!

13 Pain - it's all in the mind

Situation

JAMES: What's wrong with you? You look depressed.

REBECCA: Yes, I've got horrible toothache and I have to go to the dentist's this afternoon. And I'm terrified of dentists.

JAMES: Well, it'll soon be over – anyway there's no need to be afraid of going to the dentist's – it doesn't really hurt, you're just imagining it.

REBECCA: I'm not! Going to the dentist's is painful . . .

JAMES: And that's why you always avoid going until you've got toothache and just have to go . . .

REBECCA: I suppose so – anyway I wish they'd find a way of making it hurt less.

In the dentist's waiting room Rebecca saw an article with the title: *Pain – it's all in the mind.*

Think it over

What do you feel about going to the dentist's? Are you worried that it's going to be painful?

What is your present opinion about the statement in the title?

(a) 'It's nonsense.'
(b) 'It may be true.'
(c) 'I've no idea. I've got a completely open mind.'
(d) 'I think it's very unlikely to be true.'

Do you expect the reading passage to be scientific? sensational gossip? a story?

What do you expect from reading before you will change your mind on a question of fact like this?

Talk over incidents when you have felt physical pain – was it imagined or real?

Does the word *pain* mean the same thing if you speak about *mental pain?*

WHAT IS THE READING PURPOSE?

Do you think Rebecca would read the article?
What do you think her attitude to the title is likely to be?

(a) 'I'm sure they're right that pain is only imaginary.'
(b) 'I don't believe it.'
(c) 'I wish it were true – I hope they can convince me.'
(d) 'I'm not interested in science.'

Do you think she'll read it quickly or slowly? Carefully or just skimming?

Text

Read the passage as you think it would be read by Rebecca.

Pain - it's all in the mind

Pain is easier to endure if you know you can end it . Speakers at a session on pain at the British Association's psychology section have new evidence to support this idea for two common experiences of pain: in childbirth and at the dentist's. On the other side of the coin, their inability to control pain may explain why some people with chronic pain have psychological problems as well.

Dr J. Robinson, a psychologist at University College in Cardiff, found out about the phenomenon of self-controlled pain almost by accident. He was studying the effects of analgesics used to control pain during childbirth and as part of the experiment made it possible for women having their child to press a button which gave an automatic injection – instead of having all injections made by the doctor. Afterwards these women did not say that they had less pain than other women in childbirth, but they did use considerably less of the drug.

J. Atkins, a dental surgeon, has observed a similar phenomenon. As part of their efforts to make dentistry painless, Atkins and researchers at Aston University in Birmingham offered patients a switch they could flip to turn off the dentist's drill whenever they chose. But, after trying the switch on 50 patients Atkins gave up; none of the patients had ever flipped the switch.

Perhaps the extra endurance was because the Aston team also use other methods to make dentistry painless. Apparently few other dentists are so considerate. The end result is, according to the Birmingham survey, is that British people avoid going to the dentist, with the consequence that almost 30% of people in England and Wales have lost all their teeth, and more than seven out of ten have lost at least six teeth. Less than half of the public pay regular visits to the dentist. To find out why, Atkins and psychologist W. G. Cumberbatch interviewed a sample of patients attending a dental hospital. The most common reason people gave for not having dental check-ups were fear and pain.

By using a little care and taking time to explain what will happen, Atkins feels, dentists could overcome these fears. There are techniques for giving injections without pain, and a 'calm unhurried approach' to drilling can make that painless, too.

Sadly, few dentists seem to take much trouble with their patients. 'I am not nervous when I go to the dentist, and I do not have any pronounced sympathy for those who are,' said one dentist. 'I tend to take the point of view that they are being unreasonable at my expense.'

By Lois Wingerson, from *New Scientist*, September 4, 1980.

Do you think the passage comes from: (a) a medical textbook? (b) a psychology textbook? (c) a popular magazine? (d) a serious magazine?

Language work

A Vocabulary

(a) Does the first sentence – *pain is easier to endure if you know you can end it* – say the same thing as the title? Say the opposite of what the title says? Give an explanation of the title statement?

(b) *on the other side of the coin* means
– on the other hand
– in tact
– as a complement to this?

(c) Technical vocabulary
The text contains a number of terms connected with medicine or science: *chronic pain: phenomenon: analgesics: automatic injection*.

Use the context to guess what they mean – check with your dictionary if you are not sure.

(d) The text reports the results of a number of experiments. Find these expressions in the text.

> speakers at the British Association *have new evidence to support this idea* . . .
> Dr J Robinson *found out about* the phenomenon of self-controlled pain . . .
> J Atkins *has observed* a similar phenomenon . . .
> The result is, *according to the Birmingham survey*, that . . .

Notice how the expressions in italics are used to express the idea of what the experiment shows:

eg Dr J Robinson   *found out about*   the phenomenon of self-controlled pain.

Now use similar phrases to express the results of the following experiments.

1 The Educational Research Institute   . . . .   – 30% of children have reading problems.

2 Dr Brindle of London University   . . . .   – watching television excessively reduces reading skills.

3 Jennifer Bray, a Newcastle teacher   . . . .   – over half of British families possess fewer than ten books.

4 The Social Science Survey   . . . .   – traditional ways of learning to read are as successful as modern ways.

B Reference

1 *two common experiences of pain* (line 4) – what are they?
2 *their inability to control pain* (line 7) – who does *their* refer to?
3 *Afterwards these women* (line 19) – which women?
4 *Apparently few other dentists are so considerate* (line 32) – 'so' refers to?
5 *dentists could overcome these fears* (line 47) – which fears?
6 *I tend to take the point of view that they are being unreasonable at my expense* (line 55) – who are *they*?
7 *but they did use considerably less of the drug.* (line 20) – Why did the writer of the passage put *did use* instead of *used*?

C Comprehension

(a) What is the main *general* point made in paragraph 1?
What is the consequence of this general point?
(b) What particular instances of pain are mentioned?
(c) Paragraph 2 gives an account of an experiment:
– what was the purpose of the experiment?
– what was the experimental method?
– what were the results of the experiment?
– what general point do these results indicate?
(d) Answer the same questions for the experiment by J. Atkins.

(e) Paragraph 4 gives some approximate statistical facts about British people and their dentists – fill in the facts with the quantities.

Between 25 & 30%

Around 40 to 45%

70% or more

(f) What suggestions does Dr Atkins make to improve the situation revealed by his survey?

(g) What is the general attitude of dentists towards their patients' fear of pain?

(h) The original text was longer than the one given here. Read paragraph 1 again and say what you would expect to find in the rest of the text.

Using your reading

(a) The next day
JAMES: Hello, Rebecca – how did you get on at the dentist's?
REBECCA: Oh, terrible as usual – but you don't have to be afraid at the dentist's – I read this article in the waiting room which said . . .

Complete the conversation

(b) Write the official summary for one of the experiments described in the passage:

```
Report on Experiment
Title:                          By:

Purpose of experiment:

Subjects:

Experimental method:

Results:

Conclusions:
```

Overall understanding

In your opinion does the title – *Pain – it's all in the mind* – give a true indication of what the passage is about?

The writer of the passage mentions the names of the people who made the experiments, says where they work and how they proceeded. Why?

There are a number of possible conclusions that could be drawn from the passage. Complete what the following might be:

The British dental service needs . . .

Pain can be reduced if . . .

Dentists should . . .

Summary

In this unit you have worked on understanding accounts of scientific experiments; on reporting the results in conversation and in note form; on interpreting the conclusions to be drawn from experiments and on evaluating how writers indicate that the facts they are presenting are reliable.

14 Literacy – a right denied to 800 million

This unit – the last in the book – is rather different from most of the previous ones. It is intended to help you see how far you can apply the skills you have learnt over an extended range of information – texts, graphs, photographs and illustrations – and use it as the basis of a spoken or written report.

Situation

1978 was the Year of the Child, 1980 World Wildlife Year; 198– has been named World Literacy Year and UNESCO has organised an international collection of funds so that money is available for a campaign to teach people in Africa, Asia and South America to read and write. You have agreed to be responsible for collecting the money in the place where you work, or the school or college you study in. You want to make notes for a talk to your colleagues to explain to them the facts about literacy, why it is a problem, how you can go about dealing with the problem. You have received a lot of documents from UNESCO and you are going through them to prepare for what you want to say. Here are the headings for your notes:

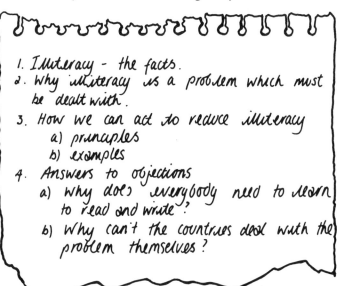

1. Illiteracy – the facts.
2. Why illiteracy is a problem which must be dealt with.
3. How we can act to reduce illiteracy
   a) principles
   b) examples
4. Answers to objections
   a) why does 'everybody' need to learn to read and write'?
   b) Why can't the countries deal with the problem themselves?

In this unit there are five different pieces of information about literacy – you should decide which information is necessary for you and put it in the relevant part of your notes.

WHAT READING STRATEGIES WILL YOU USE?

Texts

Each of the pieces of text has an exercise designed to help you process the information and judge how you can use it.

(a)

Literacy - a right denied to 800 million

The world literacy problem in the last quarter of the twentieth century could be summed up in two simple observations: as a result of colossal efforts many countries have succeeded in substantially reducing the *percentage* of illiterates in their populations; meanwhile the *absolute number* of illiterates is constantly rising because of soaring population growth.

It is estimated that if present trends are not corrected, the number of illiterates may rise from 814 million in 1980 (or approximately 1 adult in ten) to 884 million in 1990, and that mankind may enter the 21st century with at least 954 million illiterate adults.

The proportion of women in these figures is getting larger and larger. In 1960, 58% of illiterates were women; the corresponding figure today is more than 60%, and in some communities virtually the whole of the female population is illiterate.

Nearly three-quarters of the world's illiterates live in Asia, approximately 20% in Africa, and 5% in Latin America. Eleven countries have a combined illiterate population of over 400 million. Twenty-three countries have an illiteracy rate even higher than 70%. Hence the situation is serious.

. . . .

The map of illiteracy coincides with that of poverty, revealing the isolation of a large part of mankind of human groups which are at once the poorest, the worst fed and the least well-cared for.

Comprehension

1 Fact collecting – how many? who? where? when? – can you put the statistics in visual form?

2 Have previous efforts to fight illiteracy had any effect? Why is it still an enormous problem?

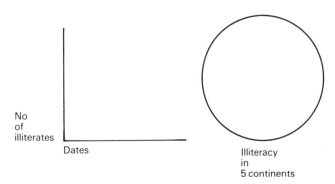

No of illiterates

Dates

Illiteracy in 5 continents

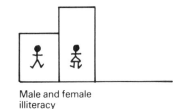

Male and female illiteracy

(b)

The adult literacy campaigns which constitute one important aspect of the action proposed by UNESCO may find helpful a number of principles which the organisation has identified from its past experience.

First of all, it is noteworthy that the most spectacular successes in adult literacy campaigns have often been achieved in a context of profound social change or in a situation of economic expansion and a broadening unemployment market. In these circumstances, literacy is regarded as a means of enabling individuals to face a new situation or to be active protagonists in bringing about the desired changes in society.

Secondly, it has become clear that literacy work can only be effective if the beneficiaries themselves participate in it, each adult becoming the agent of his or her own literacy training and being aware of the need for this personal involvement. This principle is fundamental and means that literacy work should be based on the commitment of the entire population and that it can help to strengthen its feeling of identity. Here the choice of language or languages to be used – a political decision which should be based on technical or cultural criteria – is of key importance.

A third essential principle is that of integration of literacy programmes into other developmental reforms. For example, rural development is affected by the world food crises, natural disasters and problems of under- and unemployment. Progress can only be achieved if the rural population is mobilised in the action to change things, and literacy work can be a factor in this mobilisation or a consequence of it, but its success depends on the success of other social changes.

Finally, literacy training must be followed up. Literacy and numeracy are useless accomplishments unless these basic skills are put to use in everyday life and unless the newly literate are provided with suitable material in the form of texts written in their own language which take account of their level of education and of their interests.

Reproduced from the *Unesco Courier* of June 1980.

1 What title would you give to this section of text?

2 The language here is fairly difficult and complex, but it can be summed up in a much simpler way. Here are summaries in one sentence of each paragraph. Match the summaries to the paragraphs.

(i) Literacy training only works if the people themselves know why they are learning to read and agree about its importance and the choice of language.

(ii) Literacy training won't work if people who learn to read and write have nothing provided to use their new skills with afterwards.

(iii) Literacy campaigns work best in times of economic expansion and social change.

(iv) Literacy campaigns must be associated with efforts to develop other features of people's lives and other social developments.

(c)

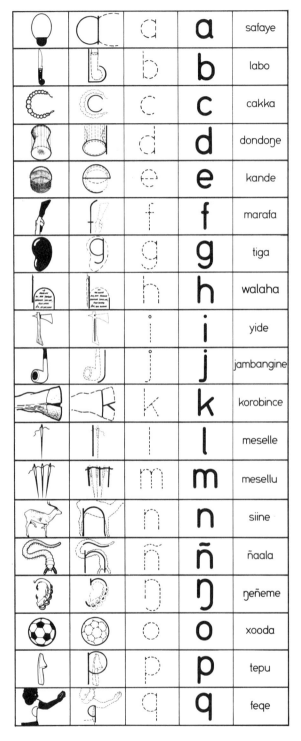

				safaye
			a	safaye
			b	labo
			c	cakka
			d	dondoŋe
			e	kande
			f	marafa
			g	tiga
			h	walaha
			i	yide
			j	jambangine
			k	korobince
			l	meselle
			m	mesellu
			n	siine
			ñ	ñaala
			ŋ	ŋeñeme
			o	xooda
			p	tepu
			q	feqe

This is a wall-chart prepared for use in a literacy campaign in Senegal in West Africa, for people who speak Mandingo, a language spoken by 3½ million people.

1 What do you think is the purpose of the wall-chart in a country where most people can't read or write?
   To teach people how . . .
   To show them that writing . . .

2 What do you think are the Mandingo words for:
   – knife?
   – drum?
   – pipe?
   – football?

3 Guess what the following words in Mandingo mean:
   – kande:
   – yide:
   – marafa:

4 Most English words form their plural by adding 's' – eg word – words. Find out from the chart one way the plural is formed in Mandingo. Guess what the plural of the word for baskets might be.

(d) **Public expenditure on education and military expenditure**
(as percentage of GNP [Gross National Product] and per inhabitant, in U.S. dollars)

		Public expenditure on education as a % of GNP	Military expenditure as a % of GNP	Public expenditure on education per inhabitant in U.S. dollars	Military expenditure per inhabitant in U.S. dollars
World total	1965	4.9	6.8	38	54
	1970	5.4	6.6	58	71
	1975	5.8	5.3	111	103
Developed countries	1965	5.2	7.5	87	127
	1970	5.6	7.1	139	176
	1975	6.0	5.5	269	246
Developing countries	1965	3.2	2.6	5	5
	1970	4.0	2.9	8	7
	1975	4.4	4.5	20	21

These figures do not include data relating to the People's Republic of China, Democratic Kampuchea, Democratic People's Republic of Korea, Lao People's Democratic Republic, South Africa and Socialist Republic of Viet Nam.

A

True (✓) or False (✗)?

1   Military expenditure fell between 1965 and 1975.   (   )
2   Developing countries in 1975 spent more on arms than on education.   (   )
3   Developed countries were, in 1975, spending relatively more on education than previously.   (   )
4   The GNPs of developed countries are on average 10 times higher than those of developing countries.   (   )
5   Each person in the world spent $103 on military expenditure in 1975.   (   )
6   By 1975 developing countries were spending more on education than on the armed forces.   (   )

B

Why has this table been put into a passage about illiteracy?
What conclusions do you draw from it?

The social causes of illiteracy

Here are five photographs. Each photograph represents one cause of illiteracy and this is explained in the caption that goes with the picture. The captions and pictures have been separated – put the right picture with the right caption.

(a) *Education imposed from outside.* Systems of education copied from other countries and which do not take into account a nation's specific conditions and needs can never be expected to come to grips with the basic problems of illiteracy.

(b) *Hunger.* So long as millions of human beings the great majority of them in the Third World are living precariously on the border-line c starvation, no educational policy, however we conceived, can by itself eradicate illiteracy.

2

(c) *Poverty.* In the developing countries, without the earnings of their school-age children, many poor families cannot even afford the basic essentials of life. Their children will grow up to swell the ranks of the great army of the illiterate.

5

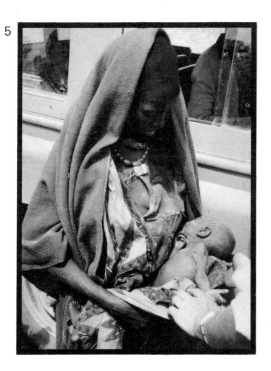

(d) *Lack of funds for education,* results in limited facilities, lack of teaching aids and the use of teachers who have not always received suitable training.

(e) *Isolation.* When a country's population is scattered, the establishment of schools and attendance at them becomes much more difficult. This problem is compounded by the fact that these isolated groups of people are amongst the poorest and the least well-fed and are unable to share in the progress of the societies to which they belong.

Caption (a) goes with photograph _____
Caption (b) goes with photograph _____
Caption (c) goes with photograph _____
Caption (d) goes with photograph _____
Caption (e) goes with photograph _____

9G10012